1 MONTH OF
FREE
READING

at

www.ForgottenBooks.com

By purchasing this book you are eligible for one month membership to ForgottenBooks.com, giving you unlimited access to our entire collection of over 1,000,000 titles via our web site and mobile apps.

To claim your free month visit:

www.forgottenbooks.com/free112500

ISBN 978-0-483-55706-2
PIBN 10112500

For support please visit www.forgottenbooks.com

LEMUEL SHAW

Chief Justice

OF THE

SUPREME JUDICIAL COURT OF MASSACHUSETTS

———————

CAMBRIDGE

JOHN WILSON AND SON

University Press

1885

THE first and second of the following biographical notices are here reprinted by permission of the New England Historic Genealogical Society and of the Hon. P. Emory Aldrich, from the series of TOWNE MEMORIAL BIOGRAPHIES published by the Society; the third, by permission of the present proprietors of the AMERICAN LAW REVIEW, being an article which originally appeared in the Review in October, 1867.

LEMUEL SHAW

EARLY AND DOMESTIC LIFE.

By SAMUEL S. SHAW. A.M., LL.B.

IN reply to the request of Christopher C. Baldwin, Esq., made on behalf of the Worcester Historical Society, that Chief Justice Shaw would furnish a copy of the sentiment given by him at the Society's celebration of the centenary of the incorporation of Worcester County, in 1831, to be enclosed with other articles in a box and kept till 1931, Judge Shaw sent, or thought of sending — time alone will tell — a summary of the events of his life up to that time, to accompany the paper asked for, a draft of which reads as follows : —

May I without unpardonable egotism seize the occasion to say a few words about myself? The hope of attracting the momentary notice of some curious antiquary of the next century must be my apology for doing so. I was born in Barnstable, January 9, 1781, was graduated at Harvard College in 1800, admitted to the Bar 1804, first in Hillsborough County, N. H., then in Plymouth County in this State, appointed Chief Justice September, 1830. My father was Oakes Shaw, graduated at Harvard 1758, ordained minister of the West Parish of Barnstable in 1760, and so continued till his death, 1807. My grandfather was John Shaw, graduated at Harvard 1729, settled as minister in the South Parish of Bridgewater, who died about 1790. His father was Joseph Shaw, a farmer and miller in East Bridgewater. My mother was Susanna Hayward of Braintree, born 1745, still living at eighty-six. Her father was John Hayward of Braintree.

I married in 1818 Elizabeth Knapp, daughter of Josiah Knapp of this city, by whom I was blessed with two children: John Oakes and Elizabeth, still living; she died June, 1822. In August, 1827, I married Hope Savage, daughter of Dr. Samuel Savage of Barnstable; we have one child, Lemuel, three years old. I commenced the practice of law in this city in the autumn of 1804, and have ever since resided here. I was a member of the House of Representatives from 1811 to 1815, again in 1819, in the Convention for amending the Constitution in 1820, in the Senate 1821–2, again in the House of Representatives in 1829. I was of the committee of the town who framed the plan of city government, drew up the report and the act of incorporation. I have held several elective offices under both the town and city government.

It may be convenient to complete this outline of facts, and to add, that another son and youngest child was born in 1833 of his second marriage, named for his grandfather Samuel Savage; that in 1834 Judge Shaw was elected Fellow of Harvard College, an office which he held till his death; that he received the degree of LL. D. from Harvard in 1831 and from Brown University in 1850; that, with the exception of an occasional illness and a vacation in Europe in 1853, his labors as judge were uninterruptedly carried on until his resignation in 1860. He died March 30, 1861. His widow survived him eighteen years and died August 13, 1879. His son Lemuel died May 6, 1884; his other children are living.

Lemuel Shaw's childhood was passed in an old-fashioned New England parsonage, if the minister's house may be so called, in that part of Barnstable known as Great Marshes. The house is still standing, though much modernized. His father was of the old style eighteenth century order of New England ministers, settled for life on a salary of £80 lawful money, afterwards increased to £100, with a certain allowance of firewood; but this stipend was sadly impaired in value during the evil period of continental paper money, and was always hard to get. Much of it was collected on orders on the Constable, agreeing to allow the amount to the Precinct Treasurer, which in the hands of the parishioner became equivalent to cash for the purpose of paying his tax. The inconvenience of this to a man with a distaste for accounts may be well imagined. For several years after the war, the Rev. Oakes Shaw seems to have maintained a chronic remonstrance against what he conceived to be the unfairness with which he was treated by the people of the Precinct in money matters, leading almost to an open rupture, which, however, happily never occurred. All this must have been very disturbing to his peace, for though active as a preacher and pastor, as testified by an obituary notice in the Panoplist, then under the direction of Dr. Jedediah Morse, business and affairs were but little to his mind. Devoting himself to his sermons and to visiting, he gladly left his worldly concerns to the management of his wife. At the time of his second marriage in 1774 to Susanna Hayward of Braintree, he was a widower with three daughters, and there were afterwards born to him two sons, John Hayward and Lemuel. It was to this excellent wife and mother that the family owed all its little measure of thrift and prosperity. She was enabled to buy the house and add to its comforts through some slight patrimony of her own.

With such parents it was natural that the education of their sons should be a matter of supreme interest. A subscription towards the charge of a school which should have a "grammar schoolmaster" of a liberal education was started by Mr. Shaw, but nothing is known to have come of it. He seems to have been the only instructor of his sons while they were at home, and to have included as their fellow-pupil the son of a neighbor, young Freeman Parker, afterwards settled at Dresden in Maine as a Congregationalist minister, whom he prepared for college gratuitously. Mr. Parker has left a pleasant reminiscence of his early days in a little poem or, as he modestly styled it, a piece of " prose run mad," written for the amusement of his grandchildren and not to be shown to any beyond the domestic circle, called " The Button-wood Tree." It is hoped that no serious violation of confidence is committed by the insertion here of the following lines.

> The button-wood tree, whose wide-spreading shade,
> Oft in the summer my study I made,
> Where Latin and Greek and English I learned,
> While thirsting for lore my young bosom burned.
> And then when prepared with heartfelt delight
> To good Father Shaw's I hied to recite.
> Well I remember his grave, solemn look,
> His three-cornered hat, his pipe, and his book.
>
> .   .   .   .
>
> I do not forget the high-backed arm-chair,
> And the old pipe-box and desk which were there
> In the study, where our lessons we said,
> And the east window with hop vines o'erspread,
> Where three of us sat learning Latin and Greek
> Day following day and week after week.

In the earliest letter, however, which we have from Lemuel, dated April 18, 1793, he writes to his brother : —

You said in your last you thought I had studied very hard, but you were much mistaken. I do not study more than half the time, my eyes are weak, and I have work to do which takes more than half the time.

From Barnstable Lemuel was sent to finish his preparation for college to the school of a Mr. Salisbury at Braintree, and on the twenty-seventh of June, 1796, his mother writes to her brother at that place : —

Lemmy writes that Mr. Salisbury's school breaks up a fortnight sooner than he expected, and wishes to know immediately what he must do. I desired Mr. Shaw to write and tell him, but he says he can't himself but has desired me to. As we expect to send this by the post I hope you will excuse me if I write to Lemmy in this sheet to save postage. . . .

In my last letter to Lemmy I told him to ask you how many bushels of rye delivered at Boston would purchase a horse-cart; as rye harvest draws near I should be glad to know. . . . If I mistake not you told me you could buy tow-cloths yard wide for 1s. per yard; if you can buy it so now I should like to have some, etc. etc.

And to Lemuel, on the other half-sheet: —

I am glad to hear you have been able to go to school every day since you have been at Braintree; no doubt your early rising contributes to your health. I am sorry your school breaks up so much sooner than you expected. If you have any encouragement from Mr. Salisbury that you would be admitted into college at Commencement your father is willing you should stay, provided your friends are willing to keep you, and you can get your present instructor or Mr. Weld to attend to hear your lessons. . . . When you are in Boston on your way home, I would have you go to the rope-walks and get a good hemp bed-cord, etc. etc.

No doubt Mr. Salisbury gave the desired encouragement, for in July Lemuel presented himself for examination at Harvard College, — with what result may be gathered from the following letters.

BARNSTABLE, August 13, 1796.

MY DEAR LEMMY, — . . . Your uncle thinks it will be of service to you that you were not admitted, and your aunt says you supported the disappointment like a man. I hope you will not be too much mortified, but will make it your endeavor to convince the government by your studious and regular conduct that you are not unworthy a place in the University if you should gain admission upon a further examination; for your further encouragement, your brother tells me of one of his classmates, who was the best scholar in the class, who was turned by for the vacation. I expect to send this by your good friend Parker, who I trust will take a fatherly care of you. I wrote you this week through the post that if my cloth was dressed that I sent by you to Weymouth you might get you a coat made this week; if it is not done, Freeman says you can obtain permission by applying to government for leave to wear such as you have by telling them how the case is circumstanced, that when you left home last May your father had no idea of your going to college this year, and that you have had no time to go home since Commencement.

Be slow and cautious in the choice of your acquaintance; in particular beware of being acquainted with the upper classes except recommended by P., or some one on whose fidelity you can depend. If possible, get some old *steady* fellow for your chum; . . . and write soon to your affectionate

MOTHER.

AUGUST 27, 1796.

MY DEAR LEMUEL, — We received by the post yesterday a letter from your good uncle Doctor, with a bond from the government of the University which announces your being admitted a member of that society. I congratulate you on the event; hope you will do honor to yourself, which will afford comfort to your friends. I trust you have a just sense of the obligation you are under to your uncles, to whose kindness and exertions you may attribute your present situation. Think what a claim they have upon you to do your best to be steady, prudent, and studious. Being forewarned is said to be forearmed; let me therefore caution you to establish a *good character*. Always beware of the first deviation from the path of rectitude. Be on your guard never to do anything privately that would cause a blush to have it exposed. I would have you go to your uncle in all cases of difficulty. . . .

Your affectionate mother,

S. S.

The uncle last mentioned was Dr. Lemuel Hayward, of Boston, whose hospitable house, on Newbury Street, opposite the White Horse, — in other words, in a garden covering nearly the whole of the present Hayward Place, — his nephew and namesake ever found a second home. No account of Lemuel Shaw would be complete without a grateful acknowledgment of the paternal care and kindness of Dr. Hayward, at all times extended to his nephew, and most valuable at his start in life, influencing, no doubt, his whole subsequent career.

And thus the youth entered the freshman class of
Harvard College, so different then from the splendidly
equipped and luxurious establishment of to-day. The
bond given for the payment of dues was conditioned in
the penalty of two hundred ounces of silver. Freshmen
fagged under the older students, and Shaw was lucky in
having his friend Parker to serve. The lean veal and
sour cider of college commons left a lasting impression on
his memory. Carpets in college rooms were unknown.
For the first year his room was at the house of a Mr.
Richard Hunnewell; afterwards in the college buildings.
His conduct seems to have been exemplary; but fines
began to be scored against him in his junior year. "For
throwing snowballs in the college yard, twenty-five cents;"
"walking on the Sabbath, one dollar," half of which was
afterwards remitted; "for entering the hall with his hat
on while the government were there, twenty-five cents,"
are among the charges. A certain amount of "exhibi-
tion" or scholarship money was allowed him. His first
vacation seems to have been passed with his uncle, the
doctor, who writes to his sister : —

Your son has been with us since the commencement of the
vacation, and has closely attended Mr. Web, his writing-master.
Agreeable to your desire, I applied to M. Duport to teach him
dancing, but he informed me that attending him five weeks only
would be of no service ; besides, his admission money would be
the same as for others, five dollars, and half a dollar a lesson,
which would make the expense for five weeks twenty dollars.
On the whole, M. Duport advised him not to enter, and I fully
joined with him in opinion, as Lemuel informs me they have a
good dancing-master at Cambridge.

And from M. Desforges at Cambridge a quarter's tuition
was received.

Of literary occupations while at college he thus wrote,
in a letter to a classmate soon after graduation : —

I should like to know whether you have been able to carry into execution that systematic plan of literary pursuits of which you used so often to be talking. Literature in my opinion is almost the only resort of a man who wishes to render his enjoyments independent of others. You will think this a singular declaration from one who seemed to care so little for the attainment of literature while in college; but I assure you my situation is now extremely altered. There I could always find some person with whom I could pass my time agreeably away; but now, though I see many different faces, and find many with whom I could associate, yet, except a very few particular friends, none with whom I could find any enjoyment.

Of the winter vacation of 1799–1800, in which he was engaged to keep the school at Lexington for the term of ten weeks at sixteen dollars per month, with board, transportation, etc., he thus wrote: —

CAMBRIDGE, February 19, 1800.

DEAR BROTHER, — . . . I have spent the winter very agreeably at Lexington, and the acquaintance I have formed in the short time that I have taught the school there I value very highly. In your letter you inquire of me what profession I expect to pursue. It is indeed a secret which I have not yet discovered myself. It in a great measure depends upon circumstances. Perhaps you have been informed that I have some prospect of employment as assistant in one of the public schools in Boston. If I do go there to assist in a school, I shall be advantageously situated for studying law. It is a profession I must confess to which I have a partiality; but you know I was always designed for the desk. From my own observation, I am fully convinced that it is not the profession that adorns the man, but the man the profession.

While in college he was elected a member of the young Phi Beta Kappa Society, then on the footing of other college societies, and at his graduation took part in a Greek dialogue.

On leaving college, a position as usher in the South Reading School, afterwards known as the Franklin School, and standing on the site of the present Brimmer School, was obtained; and here, as he afterwards expressed it, he "worried through" a year. But though regarded by himself as a year of vexation, drudgery, and failure to maintain discipline, yet we are told that Master Bullard spoke of him in the politest manner, and said he was the best usher that was ever in the school since he knew it.

His mother, writing on February 26, 1801, says : —

You seem to be undetermined as to the choice of a profession. I hope you will not be left to mistake your talent. I could name several that took upon them the sacred profession of divinity, their profession so far from regulating their conduct that their conduct would have disgraced a Hottentot. Others we have seen in various professions who have been an ornament to the Christian religion. I was not aware till I had just finished the last sentence that you might construe it into a discouragement of entering upon the study of divinity. This was not my intention, for I do most sincerely hope that you will make it your study through life, whether you ever preach or not. I hope you will remember that you are not to look to yourself alone, but to others also. I conceive it to be your duty to provide for yourself in that way in which you are capable of doing the most good and being the most extensively useful. In order to promote so desirable an end it may be best for you to take some more time to consider the subject, at the same time to be as diligent as health and circumstances will permit to lay up a stock of general knowledge that may be useful to you in future, let your particular calling be what it may. I hope you will not suffer yourself to give way to discouragement. Our country is very extensive; there is ample space for all good men of every profession. Seek first and principally the kingdom of heaven and the righteousness thereof, and you need not fear but that all other things that Infinite Wisdom shall see to be best for you shall be added to you.

"You are then liberated from your hated cage," writes his college chum, Timothy Boutelle, on September 6, 1801; and about this time Mr. Shaw entered as a student the office of Mr. David Everett, a lawyer at Boston. Judge

Thomas, in his interesting notice in the Law Review for October, 1867, has spoken slightingly of this gentleman, but Dr. Hayward had a high opinion of his professional ability and character, and young Shaw felt under great obligation to him. Mr. Everett spoke of his pupil in the highest terms, and said he bade fair to make a great figure. He gave his pupil plenty to do. " You tell me," says Boutelle, in 1801, " that you expect soon to enter the lists with justice lawyers. It would gratify me indeed if I could come incog. and hear some of your frothy spoutations."

Under date of April 16, 1802, he writes his mother : —

Court sits here next week. Mr. Everett must of course attend. The office must not be deserted. Court will continue three or four weeks. I should like to go home ; but as my studies are very much interrupted by business, I must avoid all extra avocations ; besides, I am now trying to make farther proficiency in the French language under the instruction of M. Renaud. Interest and inclination require that I should give it my closest attention.

The immediate result of M. Renaud's instructions was an attempt at translating a work for the press ; and in December, 1802, there appeared " Proposals by Russell and Cutler for publishing by subscription a new work entitled A Political and Historical View of the Civil and Military Transactions of Bonaparte, First Consul of France. Translated from the French of J. Chas, to be put in press as soon as five hundred copies are subscribed for at one dollar." The translation was completed, but not the subscription list; though the book seems to have been not badly chosen for a venture of the kind, at a moment when the fortunes of Europe and the world were rapidly becoming identified with those of its subject. Whatever may have been the young translator's disappointment on this occasion, it was soon forgotten in the more engrossing interest of his professional studies, and in a removal

to Amherst, New Hampshire, with his friend Everett, who
opened an office there. At about the same time his
French teacher returned to his native land, there to resume his true name of Antoine Jay, and to commence
a distinguished career in politics and literature. As
one of the founders of the Constitutionnel newspaper he
acquired wealth, and his literary performances were rewarded with a chair in the French Academy. In the
year 1841 he wrote to the Chief Justice a most friendly
letter, which, as containing his reminiscences of Boston
in 1801–1802, seems deserving of preservation : —

(*Translation.*)

PARIS, April 16, 1841.

MY DEAR SIR, — . . . I have seen the time when it would
have been as easy to write you in English as in French, but
that time is far distant. The English language is still familiar
to me, but I no longer write or speak it with the same ease as
when I counted you among my most intelligent pupils. That
period has left in my memory agreeable recollections, during
the course of a laborious life, which has rolled on rapidly in
the midst of excitements and of the most astounding political
revolutions. I have often regretted the serene days and peace-
ful nights of my sojourn at Boston, when I found myself so
fortunate in my social and, I may venture to say, friendly relations with the most eminent men and the most respected families of your flourishing city. The American manners, then so
elegant in their simplicity, agreed with my character, and it was
not without effort that I tore myself, in 1803, from that hospitable land where, a poor exile, I had found sympathy and
protection. To this day, in my solitary reveries my imagination retraces the places where I lived, the persons whom I
knew, during my long residence at Boston. In thought I stroll
through your populous streets, over your wharves piled with
the products of all parts of the world. I transport myself to
Beacon Hill, to enjoy the spectacle so magnificent and so varied,
of your harbor and roadstead, of the islands with which it is
strewn, and the numerous vessels that cover and adorn it. I
have forgotten neither the promenade of the Mall, nor the cele-

brated Dorchester Heights, nor the Mystic River, nor Bunker Hill, consecrated by the glorious deaths of the first heroes of Independence. And so, of all the works of Cooper, Lionel Lincoln is the one which I have read with most interest, and solely because Boston is the scene of action which he has chosen.

After remarks upon the future of the United States, for which he entertained fears, and upon the unsettled political condition of France, M. Jay says : —

I know not what the future has in reserve for us, but I should not be surprised if, at my advanced age, I should be forced a second time to go and ask the hospitality of the people of the United States. Assuredly I should not hesitate a single instant to do so, and Boston would again be the place I should choose for my last asylum.

Student life in Boston was cheered by some very intimate friendships, especially by those of Eben Appleton, a brother of the more widely known Nathan and Samuel, and of John A. Cumming, of the Harvard class of 1801. For the former, afterwards long separated by his residence in the South and in England, Shaw entertained a tender affection, which he expressed in a gracefully worded obituary notice. The three "merry men," as Appleton styled himself and friends, gave each other Shakespearian nicknames, Appleton being called Falstaff; Cumming, Hal; and Shaw, Bardolph. This club of three seems to have been literary so far as contributions of prose and verse to the Commercial Gazette· may entitle it to that character, and to its youthful gaiety the effervescing spirits of Appleton must have contributed the largest share. Shaw's removal to Amherst did not interrupt the intercourse or amusements of the young men. There were cultivated families there, and a good deal of young and gay society. Appleton had connections in the town, and visited there. A newspaper called the Cabinet had just been started by an enterprising young man,

Joseph Cushing, who was happy to receive the communications of aspirants to authorship. Here, too, was formed an attachment, resulting in an engagement to a daughter of Major Thomas Melvill, of Boston, with whose family Mr. Shaw was ever after on the most intimate terms. This engagement was broken by the early death of the young lady. Herman Melville, the author, a grandson of Major Melvill, subsequently married a daughter of Judge Shaw.

But the dances and sleighing parties of Amherst could furnish no aid in deciding the momentous question where to go when the duly admitted counsellor-at-law should be thrown out into the world. On July 20, 1804, he writes: —

I have thought of about fifty different places to settle in, I have calculated the advantages and disadvantages, which last indeed generally preponderate, and am still as much at a loss as ever. One thing, however, I am fully determined on, that is, not to determine at all until I have had an opportunity to consult those who feel an interest in my welfare and at the same time are capable of advising me. If I have a favorable opportunity, I think it probable I may go to Boston in the course of a few days to see my uncle whom I wish very much to converse with.

His admission to the Bar of Hillsborough County took place in September, 1804, and to that of Plymouth County, Massachusetts, in October following.

The beginning of 1805 found him in an office in Boston on Congress Street, of which he says: "The tenements in this street are not numbered, but you may easily distinguish my office by this description, 'adjoining Russell and Cutler's printing office.'" His business was, very much as he expected, very small. The tedium of waiting was alleviated that winter by the continued course of fine sleighing which he "improved considerably," and by an introduction for the first time to the

Boston Assembly, a scene of splendor and elegance, which, being attended by some very good company of his acquaintance, he enjoyed highly. Employment, however, began to come in this first year, not so profitable, however, as to render an expected vacancy in a clerkship of the New Hampshire Court unattractive to his attention and inquiries. In December he moved into the office of Mr. Thomas O. Selfridge, on the north side of the Old State House, and became very busy. On August 4, 1806, occurred the shooting of young Charles Austin by Mr. Selfridge, in whose innocence and ultimate acquittal Mr. Shaw believed from the first. "Constant employment" now became "a weight of business," for the time being at least.

But during the earlier years of his professional life, he had to struggle against a natural tendency to indolence, of which no one was better aware than himself. On March 9, 1808, he writes to his mother in apology for not writing before: "It is not to be dissembled, I cannot deceive myself in this particular, that I am under the influence of an unconquerable, or rather I hope not unconquerable, but a strong and inveterate habit of procrastinating and postponing till to-morrow what ought to be done to-day." This he accounted for on the ground of his pursuits not being of a nature to compel a regular distribution of his time. "I sometimes postpone engagements," he says, "till they accumulate and press upon me so as to produce extreme uneasiness and anxiety. I then rouse up with resolution and activity and propose a thorough amendment, and go on until I have discharged most of my obligations so as to feel at ease, and then go over the same routine. I hope and resolve to improve in this particular and establish for myself a more regular distribution of time and employment, and adhere to it with more firmness. I even have the satisfaction to think I have done something towards amendment." In the course of a tour made in 1808 through Albany, Hudson, and the State of Connecticut, he went on board of "Fulton's celebrated steamboat, a wonderful machine of one hundred and sixty feet long, calculated to accommodate eighty passengers with beds, and many other accommodations in the most splendid style."

In the year 1811, Mr. Shaw was invited to deliver the annual discourse before the Humane Society. In it he touched upon the growing philanthropy of the age, the partial abolition of the slave-trade, the prospect of a suitable asylum for lunatics, — a subject which he says had been pressed with such earnestness that cold, cautious and calculating men could not avoid suspecting some sinister purpose in it, — on resuscitation and life-boats; and indulged in the following bit of Anti-Bonapartism, none the less sincere though it was good federal politics :

It is the misfortune of the present age to witness the most tremendous experiments upon the flexibility of human character that the world has ever exhibited. In alluding to the ferocious despotism that has desolated the fairest portions of Europe, let me earnestly hope that no party feeling will be imputed to me. God forbid that on this solemn occasion I should cherish or impart an ungenerous prejudice so inauspicious to its design. But as the humble advocate of the cause of humanity, whose interests are this day intrusted to my charge, it is impossible not to feel and it would be a dereliction of duty not to express the deepest abhorrence of a despotism equally at war with the dictates of justice, the precepts of religion, and the rights of humanity. Struggling for the preservation of life, shall we patiently see the lives of millions of innocents sacrificed without remorse to satiate the rapacity of individual ambition ?

In the year 1813, Mr. Shaw became one of the original board of directors of the New England Bank and retained his office till his appointment to the Bench, acting also as counsel to that institution.

His Fourth of July Oration in 1815, delivered while the result of the last struggle of the great disturber of the world's peace was unknown to the auditors, after an historical sketch of the events leading to independence, while paying an enthusiastic tribute to the successes of our navy in the recent war, was unsparing in its denunciations of the French policy of the Democratic administrations and earnest in its warning against the dangers arising from French domination in Europe.

In June, 1816, he accompanied a party of friends, among whom were several distinguished men, including Dr. Jacob Bigelow and Dr. Francis Boott, afterwards of London, on an expedition to the White Mountains and an ascent of Mount Washington. The following letter presents a curious contrast between then and now.

CONWAY, N. H., June 30, 1816.

MY DEAR MOTHER, — The mail going only once a week from this place I know not whether this will reach you sooner than my return, but believing it possible that it may, and knowing that you will be anxious to hear from me, I shall write a short letter to take its chance. We have hitherto proceeded very pleasantly, and without any incident or impediment. We went through Concord to Hanover, New Hampshire, and joined our friends whom we found there on Tuesday. The next day proceeded forward up Connecticut River as far as Lancaster and thence in an easterly and southeasterly direction to this place, which we reached a few hours since. We have ridden for the last three days in sight of the White Mountains, of which we have had a great variety of grand and magnificent views at different points of view. We propose commencing the grand operation of ascending them to-morrow morning, and expect to be engaged the greater part of three days in effecting it. As the ascent is described to us, it will probably be attended with some considerable labor and fatigue, but not more than I had prepared myself to expect. We shall be furnished with guides and men to assist us in carrying our provisions and baggage, and shall therefore undergo as little labor as the nature of the undertaking will admit. We yesterday passed through the celebrated natural passage through the mountains known by the name of the Notch. Having always greatly admired wild mountain scenery, I expected to be highly gratified by the views which this grand and curious spot presents. But I confess the reality very much surpassed my expectations, highly as they were raised. The immense height and steepness of the adjoining mountains, the narrowness of the passage, the extreme ruggedness of the immense masses of impending and projecting rock, all together give to it a character more striking and grand than I had imagined. We have found ourselves better accommodated on the way than I expected, particularly in those remote parts of the country where there are but few inhabitants and very little travelling to encourage public houses. We are now in a more settled town at Mrs. McMillan's, where everything appears neat and comfortable. I find my companions, as I expected to do, in every respect agreeable men, equally distinguished by their intelligence, their scientific attainments, and affable manners. I have now no doubt of getting home about the time proposed, the beginning of next week. Remember me in suitable terms to all my friends, and believe me truly your affectionate son,

LEMUEL SHAW.

On his marriage in 1818 to Miss Eliza Knapp, he commenced housekeeping at Number 7 Kneeland Street, in one of a row of houses built by his father-in-law, Mr. Josiah Knapp, a well-known citizen of what was then called the South End, where he continued to reside till his removal to Sumner afterwards Mount Vernon Street, in 1831. He had previously for some time been domesticated under the hospitable roof of his intimate friends, Mr. and Mrs. Daniel P. Parker.

Of his part in the Constitutional Convention of 1820, and of his work in association with Mr. Metcalf of preparing an edition of the Statutes, Judge Thomas has sufficiently written. In regard to the charter of the City of Boston, it may be added that its author considered the election of aldermen, as representing the former selectmen, from the city at large, to be an essential feature of the system, as much so as the principle of local representation recognized in the composition of the council.

It is well known that before the manufacturing interests of New England had obtained a controlling influence in the politics of that region there were movements in favor of a free-trade policy, which were supported by a large and respectable part of the community, who did not afterwards follow the cause into the Democratic camp, where it found shelter and advocacy. Of these friends of free trade Mr. Shaw was one, and he took an active part in promoting the doctrine. He was at the head of a committee appointed at a meeting of Boston merchants and others, held in January, 1829, in opposition to the tariff then recently established, and prepared a Memorial to Congress, which, according to the Free Trade Advocate of Philadelphia, "is written with a master's hand, and cannot fail to be admired for the force of its reasoning, the temperate language in which it is expressed, and the taste displayed in its composition."

The death of Isaac Parker, Chief Justice of the Supreme Judicial Court, in July, 1830, was a very sudden and unexpected event, as he had previously enjoyed uninterrupted health, and died at the age of sixty-two, after an illness of only twenty hours. Nothing could therefore have been less anticipated than an appointment to the office thus left vacant. Around the visit of Daniel Webster, who came to persuade his acceptance of this place, Judge Thomas, following a popular tradition, has thrown a cloud of smoke, by no means unlikely to have accompanied a deliberation so profoundly serious as that in which the object of these highly flattering exertions was then engaged. But it should be added that the habit of smoking was soon after this event completely abandoned. The following memorandum and letters give the main facts of the transaction : —

Memorandum.

Whether I shall accept the appointment of Judge.

AGAINST IT : —

I shall in some measure sacrifice ease and independence ; it will be more laborious. I shall lose something in part of present emolument. I shall be more absent from my family at a time when my presence might be useful to my children. I shall miss the opportunity of travelling, of making tours and journeys, and be confined principally to the pale of the Commonwealth.

IN FAVOR : —

Although I shall have a good deal of labor I do not know that is more irksome — in many respects it is less so — than that of the Bar. There will be considerable intervals of leisure. Although the emolument will not be so great as that which I have been receiving, yet it is more regular, permanent, and secure.

At fifty the labors of the Bar begin to become irksome, and many a man who has in early life enjoyed a full practice is apt to decline after that period.

The situation is a highly honorable and useful one, which, if the duties of it are ably and acceptably discharged, will lay the foundation of an honorable lasting name.

The above "if" is with me the great cause of apprehension and alarm.

Upon this I confess I am influenced more by the judgment of others than my own. I am conscious that I cannot thus discharge the duties ; they assure me that I can. I have only one consolation, that I have often thought the same in regard to other arduous undertakings and yet upon trial have found my strength equal to the occasion. If I undertake this great office, God grant it may be so here.

AUGUST 23.

MY DEAR SIR, — I am really *grieved* by your note. Would you not take the subject into consideration till to-morrow or next day and let the nomination be suspended ? Yours truly,

D. WEBSTER.

To his Wife.

23d AUGUST, 1830.

MY DEAR H., — Never have I wanted to see you so much as to-day. I am extremely perplexed by a direct offer of the office of Chief Justice. Mr. Webster called on me last evening with a message from the Governor to that effect. This morning I peremptorily declined. But afterwards I received a farther communication, and I believe the nomination is postponed till to-morrow. I have given the subject the deepest attention. The considerations are very strong on both sides. I must decide to-day. It is a most important crisis in my life. I should be extremely glad if I could have your advice. But as I cannot, must decide without. . . .

24 AUGUST, 1830.

MY DEAR H., — The deed is now done. I have been nominated to-day by the Governor as Chief Justice, and nothing remains but to make every exertion and preparation to discharge the new and arduous duties which this office will impose.

25 AUGUST, 1830.

MY DEAR H., — My nomination was announced in the papers this morning. I have received many congratulations on the subject. I am assured, in a manner which I believe to be sincere, that the appointment will give satisfaction. These are very gratifying proofs of confidence and regard, but those who give them know little of the solicitude and anxiety which I feel on the subject.

Chief Justice Shaw first took his seat at the September Term of 1830 for Berkshire, and then delivered an address commemorative of his predecessor, incidentally introducing an historical sketch of the constitution of the court, a useful contribution to the scanty history of our state tribunals.

His published charge to the Grand Jury for Essex in May, 1832, was the last which the Supreme Court had occasion to deliver to a Grand Jury, owing to changes in the law.

In 1834 he was called to preside at the capital trial of the Convent Rioters, whose high-handed outrage had behind it the sympathetic approval of a large but unenlightened part of the community. It is satisfactory to know that in his dealing with this and other cases where the hostility of differing religions embittered the questions at issue, he retained the confidence of all parties. On his retirement from the Bench he received a letter from the Roman Catholic Bishop of Boston, expressing his share in the general regret that the Commonwealth and its citizens were no longer under the protection of " the triple shield of his profound jurisprudence, his calm wisdom, and his incorruptible justice ;" and, after recalling the " know-nothing " legislation of a few years previous, which had alarmed his people, he adds : —

Allow me to say, honorable sir, that I was disturbed by no such feeling ; and the reason was because I knew that the Honorable Lemuel Shaw was at the head of the Judiciary, and that despite of prevalency or power of party the cause of justice and of right was safe in his hands.

To this conviction I gave utterance many a time ; and I now ask permission to say the same to you, not in flattery but in the very sincerity of truth. Wishing you every blessing and happiness I beg you to accept the assurance of my most profound respect. Your obedient servant,

JOHN B. FITZPATRICK,
Bishop of Boston.

The salary of the Chief Justice at the time of his appointment was three thousand five hundred dollars, that of his associates three thousand dollars, and so remained till the year 1843, when the Democratic Legislature of that year, applying the pruning-knife of supposed reform, made a general reduction in the pay of State officers, not even sparing the judges. It was thought that the Chief Justice had been receiving too much by five hun-

dred dollars, and of this amount he was to be deprived.
He would have been something more than human not to
have felt this keenly as a strictly personal matter, but as
such he never would have brought his private feelings
before the public in the shape of a formal protest addressed to the Legislature.   In the vindication, however,
of what he regarded as a constitutional principle he did
prepare such a protest, which contained an amount of
self-reference very unusual in him and presumably very
little to his taste.   In the manuscript draft of his reply to
the Committee of the Bar, which waited upon him on his
retirement from the Bench, the following passage is
found, not contained in the newspaper report.   If it was
not then read, in all probability mature reflection induced
him to leave the whole matter in oblivion, lest he might
seem to be airing an old private grievance, long before
amply redressed.   Speaking of the " gusts and whirl-
winds of political violence," he says : —

I think I may refer without any invidious allusion to an incident which has occurred since I have held my judicial appointment.   It suited the views of a dominant party to endeavor to
gain favor with the people by a scheme of economy consisting
mainly of the reduction of salaries and, to give it an air of impartiality, to extend it to the salaries of the Judges of the Supreme Judicial Court.   On this occasion I prepared an address
to be presented to the House of Representatives stating the
reasons why it should not pass, not because it affected my interest but because it was contrary to reason and justice, to the
spirit of the Constitution and, as I thought, to the best policy
of the Commonwealth.   It happened that I had prepared the
paper on the very evening on which a stormy debate arose in
the House, which resulted in the adoption of the measure.   It
seemed then worse than useless to address such a paper to
such a body before the sober sense of the community had time
to regain the ascendant.   That such a time would sooner or
later occur I had no doubt, and I may add that within one
year the obnoxious measure was repealed.

Not only was the measure repealed but the former salaries were restored with arrears at the former rate, and
until this restoration his salary in fact remained undrawn.

The address spoken of argued that the provision of the
Constitution which declared that permanent and honorable salaries should be established by law for the Justices
of the Supreme Judicial Court, which might be enlarged
if found insufficient, meant a fixed compensation in money
as distinguished from fees, casual profits, temporary grants,
and all other varying and fluctuating modes of payment;
and that the provision for an increase without mention of
a diminution afforded a strong implication against any
power to diminish. When, therefore, a judge had ac-
cepted an office on tenure of good behavior, to which
was annexed a salary established under an express injunction of the Constitution, there seemed to be all the
elements of a compact by which he was entitled to receive such salary so long as he should continue to per-
form all the duties of this office. In the Constitutional
Convention of 1820 it had been proposed to leave the
whole matter to the Legislature, also to introduce into
the Constitution an express power to lessen salaries, also
to fix a *maximum* and *minimum* ; all which changes had
been deliberately rejected. The power to fix salaries
prospectively, to take effect on new appointments, was
not questioned. As a matter of expediency, he then
went on to say, no man is competent to be a judge, who
has not been a successful practitioner, and as such able
to command the highest professional rewards ; and, if
withdrawn from such prospects, he should receive a
compensation, not indeed equal to the emolument he re-
linquishes, but an honorable and permanent provision sufficient to enable him to live in the society to which he
has been accustomed, to support his family, and educate
his children. The paper concluded with a reference to
himself.

I have no hesitation in expressing my unqualified belief that during the whole period that I have been in office, my income from professional services with less arduous and continued labor would have been more than double the income I have received from the State. I may then be asked why I relinquished the higher income to accept my present office. The answer, I trust, will commend itself to every honorable and ingenuous mind. Beyond an honorable and permanent provision for support emolument is not the only good or the greatest good. I regarded the office as a highly honorable one, as much so as any to which a professional man in a free community can aspire, and one in which useful and faithful public service is duly appreciated and liberally acknowledged and rewarded. It was one which I knew had commanded the respect and affection of the people, and which I had no doubt would command their respect and affection unless forfeited by misconduct. These were my inducements for accepting the office so kindly but unexpectedly conferred upon me, and I may say with entire sincerity that though it involved some sacrifice of pecuniary interest I have never for a moment regretted it. . . .

And in conclusion I would say that I feel a deeper interest in this subject on account of its relations to the judicial establishment and the permanent character and interests of the Commonwealth than on account of the personal interest which I have in it, though it is only in consequence of having such personal interest that I should feel at liberty to address the two houses of the Legislature on the subject.

The most celebrated criminal trial over which Judge Shaw ever presided was that of Professor Webster for the murder of Dr. Parkman. Time seems to have vindicated his impartiality and ability on that occasion, but at the moment he was assailed by savage attacks in the newspapers of New York and Philadelphia, and by abusive letters. This is a specimen paragraph taken from the New York Globe in relation to the so-called "infamous charge" : —

Pusillanimity, or prejudice, or something worse, had swerved him from the path of judicial integrity. Out of Massachusetts, and out of a limited circle in it, his judicial character is prostrated, and he will be the first of American judges associated, in position and character, with the band of cruel and corrupt English judges of whom Jeffreys is foremost, and he will be without their extenuating claim of the bias and necessities of political and party requirement.

The writer was, however, wrong in his statement as to public opinion out of Massachusetts. The eminent Daniel Lord, of New York, wrote for the express purpose of assuring Judge Shaw that, among those whose judgment he would value, the conduct and result of the trial were admired as honorable to the court, the Bar, and the people of the State. He said : —

In my recent attendance at the Court of Appeals I conversed with some of the judges, with our late Chief Justice, and with other gentlemen of the highest professional rank there as well as here, and but one opinion existed among them, — that the conduct of this trial by the court and jury had rendered Massachusetts a model to her sister States and an honor to the country.

Among the reasons which had occurred to him for declining the appointment of Chief Justice was that he would miss the opportunity of travelling, and be confined to the pale of the Commonwealth, which shows the keenness of his enjoyment of new scenes and an increased knowledge of the world. His observation was very accurate and his knowledge of localities remarkable. He had much fondness for natural history and an open mind for interesting facts in all departments of human knowledge; and for a busy professional man of his time he saw a good deal of the world. Besides journeys to Niagara and Canada and elsewhere, he visited Washington in 1841, went to Chicago by way of the lakes in 1845, and highly enjoyed a vacation in Europe in 1853. From his letters from abroad the following extracts are taken : —

STEAMSHIP ARABIA, AT SEA, June 20, 1853.

The retirement of the private cabin affords ample time for reflection, and the circumstances attending it constantly present subjects for reflection. Our feelings and affections for wife, children, home, and friends may be always strong, always abiding ; in the ordinary events of daily life, its common and customary pursuits and occupations are so uniform and so much alike that there is nothing to call for any concentration of them to one point or any express manifestation ; but on leaving home for a considerable time, and for a long distance, the heart is made conscious at once of the existence and strength of these affections, without which life would be a blank. In being made to realize that the crowning and pervading joy of life is love, and that without it imagination, learning, powers of mind are all in vain, we are made wise, and taught the true source of all happiness.

LONDON, July 1, 1853.

. . . We have employed three days very diligently and successfully. I can hardly enumerate the things we have done in regular order. Thursday was a very busy day. Baron Alderson, to whom I had a letter from Mr. Lawrence, called on me in the evening, and informed me that the judges, by request of the House of Lords, were in attendance there, hearing a law argument, and requested us, L. and myself, to come down any time in the course of the forenoon, send in a card by the officer, and he would come and introduce us. We walked down across St. James's Park, passed through Westminster Hall, and into the House of Lords. We saw there many of the distinguished personages of the kingdom, and were introduced to several of them. . . . In the evening L. and myself went to Baron Alderson's by invitation, and there met a small party of ladies and gentlemen. The house and arrangements in all respects, and the conduct of all parties, were very much the same as we might expect at the house of a respectable family in our own place.

LONDON, July 12, 1853.

We left London on Saturday morning for Oxford, to attend a dinner given by the High Sheriff on occasion of opening the commission for the assizes, in other words, of the courts sitting there. We had an invitation, through some of L.'s London friends, to take up our abode in one of the colleges, it being now vacation at the University. We left London between nine and ten in the morning, by railroad to Oxford, and arrived there, about sixty miles, between twelve and one o'clock. We proceeded at once to Brasenose College, where two nice college rooms had been provided for us, each with a well-furnished sitting-room and a small bed-room adjoining; but everything old, antiquated in the extreme, full as old in all its arrangements as S.'s room in Old Massachusetts. We were the guests of Mr. Chaffers, Vice-Principal of Brasenose, who was not there when we first went, but arrived in the course of the day. We, that is, L. and myself, went about and saw many of the ancient halls and colleges; and after Mr. C., our London friend, arrived, we went to many others, and visited the Radcliffe Library and Bodleian Library as places of special interest. At six o'clock we went to the dining-hall, which is a large hall belonging to the city of Oxford, and lent to the Sheriff for the occasion. The Sheriff, Mr. Morell, is a very wealthy man belonging to Oxford, and had invited the magistrates and leading men of the county, including many of the barristers in attendance on the courts, and many of the distinguished men of the University, and members of Parliament. After the cloth was removed, toasts were given and speeches made, in several of which I was alluded to as an American judge and stranger of distinction; and at last my health was drunk in such a manner that it was impossible to avoid rising to return thanks for the honor, which of course I did. What I said was received with all external marks of favor and satisfaction. In the course of the evening, before the dinner and in the hall, I was introduced to many persons of distinction, and was placed at the table between two members of Parliament. So ended the Sheriff's dinner at Oxford. The judges did not attend, it being regarded as contrary to the rules of etiquette for the judges to accept an invitation of the Sheriff.

His tour on the Continent was the ordinary but delightful one of Holland, the Rhine, Switzerland, and Paris, taken with pleasure, but with an ever-increasing desire for home, where he arrived safely, in the middle of September, there to resume his regular labors for the remaining seven years of his life.

Though not one of those precise persons whose time is exactly parcelled out, he was a continuous and steady worker, filling up all the available gaps which his engagements in court left him, in the writing of opinions, — his usual occupation of an evening continued frequently till midnight.

But while this never-ending task went on, he found much social recreation in the Friday-Evening Club, the Law Club, and the meetings of the trustees of the old Boston Library, at all of which the company sat down to a supper at about nine in the evening, a custom now almost, if not entirely, obsolete.

He was a member of many learned societies. His admission to the New England Historic Genealogical Society was as an honorary member in January 25, 1847.

In the year 1860, having then nearly attained the age of eighty, and completed thirty years of service, being in the full possession of his mental and bodily faculties, he tendered his resignation as Chief Justice. It was received with a universal expression of respect and affection from the public; and the address of a committee of the Bar of the whole State gave him the opportunity of making a farewell address, in which he feelingly acknowledged the support which his reliance on the good-will of his professional associates, the advocates at the Bar, had furnished him, and in which he left his testimony to the value of our judicial system : —

Above all, let us be careful how we disparage the wisdom of our fathers in providing for the appointment to judicial office, in fixing the tenure of office, and making judges as free, impartial, and independent as the lot of humanity will admit. Let no plausible or delusive hope of obtaining a larger liberty, let not the example of any other State, lead you in this matter to desert your own solid ground until cautious reason or the well-tried experiments of others shall have demonstrated the establishment of a judiciary wiser and more solid than our own.

Though no warning of an approaching end had at the time of his resignation been given, it seemed afterwards as if that step had been exactly timed in view of the short season that remained to him to complete unfinished work and set his house in order. He had long been a sufferer from annual hay fever, and in the autumn of 1860 the asthmatic symptoms of that disease seemed to linger on beyond the regular period. These and other indications were not long after considered by his physicians as showing an affection of the heart, not of an immediately alarming nature. During the course of the winter he was confined to the house, and led a life of some discomfort, but not of pain, busying himself with his arrears of opinions for the Reporter and with some professional work on which his advice was sought. On the twenty-ninth of March, 1861, he drove out to take the air, and was at dinner with his family. Not long after, the wandering of his mind showed that a change had come, and after a night of disturbed sleep, he passed away, gently and without suffering, on the morning of the thirtieth. His largely attended funeral took place at the New South meeting-house, in Summer Street, on the third of April, in the midst of one of the severest snow-storms of the year. His remains are buried in Mount Auburn Cemetery.

In religious opinion he was in sympathy with the Unitarians of his day; but his religion did not express itself so much in confident assertion of what he considered the truth as in the elevation and purity of his thoughts and aims, his strict integrity, and his many generous acts of kindness. That the devotional mood was not unknown to him, however, is shown by several written prayers found among his papers. The following one was written at sea, on his voyage to Europe : —

Almighty God, maker alike of the vast ocean and of the solid land, author and creator of all worlds, I thank Thee that in the midst of the great deep I am not beyond the reach of Thy constant notice and of Thy paternal and beneficent regard ; that I am permitted, humbly and with filial confidence, to approach Thee, to love Thee as a father, and to adore Thee as a God. Our Heavenly Father, the father of my human intelligent soul, who hath invested us with all the powers and faculties we possess, may we at all times and in all places, in danger as well as in safety, in sorrow as in joy, look to Thee for protection, preservation, and mercy. It is Thou, our father and preserver, who hast indued us with intelligence, filled our souls with the capacity of loving and the joy of being loved, who hast inspired us with hope. Oh, enable us, we beseech Thee, to enlarge and strengthen this hope until it shall ripen into a perfect confidence and faith in Thee and in Thy love for us.

LEMUEL SHAW

PROFESSIONAL AND JUDICIAL LIFE.

By HON. P. EMORY ALDRICH, LL.B.

THE writer has been requested to prepare a brief sketch of the " professional and judicial career of Chief Justice Shaw." The prescribed limits of this sketch will make anything beyond a general outline of the subject impossible.

The professional and judicial life of the Chief Justice extended over a period of fifty-six years, — twenty-six years at the Bar and thirty years on the Bench. His published opinions are found in fifty-five volumes of the Massachusetts Reports, beginning with the tenth of Pickering and ending with the fifteenth of Gray. These opinions are numerous and embrace every branch of the law, both civil and criminal, and many of them deal with the most important questions of Constitutional law.

Before his elevation to the Bench, he had won a reputation for that profound knowledge of the law in all its departments, which at once justified his appointment to the exalted position which had been occupied by the illustrious Parsons, and gave to the judiciary of the State a judge entitled to an equal place among the most eminent magistrates who have adorned the judicial annals of our country.

After graduating at Harvard College in the class of 1800, he devoted one year to teaching in one of the public schools of Boston. He then began the study of law,

and was admitted to the bar in 1804. He opened an
office in Boston, and continued in practice there till his
appointment as Chief Justice of the Supreme Judicial
Court in 1830.

His advancement in the profession could not have
been very rapid at first, as he did not argue his first case
before the Supreme Judicial Court until 1810, six years
after his admission to the Bar. This case may be found
reported in the sixth volume of Massachusetts Reports.
The amount involved was only five dollars, and the future
Chief Justice lost his case; although, as the court gra-
ciously said in deciding against him, he argued " fully
and ingeniously" in support of his writ of error to re-
verse the judgment against his client. One of his last
cases before leaving the Bar, was that of Charles River
Bridge *vs.* Warren Bridge, twice reported: first, in 6
Pickering; second, in 7 Pickering. This was one of the
most important cases which, up to that time, had been
prosecuted in our courts. The questions involved were
numerous, touching the jurisdiction of the courts, the
forms of procedure, the right of eminent domain, and
the constitutional powers of the legislature.

The discussion of these questions before the court excited great interest and no little feeling at the time, not
only among the members of the profession but throughout the State. The cause was twice argued by Mr.
Shaw, with a wealth of learning and forensic ability that
have been rarely surpassed. The court, then consisting
of only four judges, was equally divided on the main
question; but in order that the case might be carried to
the Supreme Court of the United States, for a final decision of the constitutional questions upon which the rights
of the parties depended, the bill was by order of the
court dismissed; which judgment was not affirmed by
the Federal court until 1837, nearly ten years after the
commencement of the suit in the State court.

The cause was first argued in the Supreme Court of the United States in 1836, and, having been held under advisement by that court for a year, was, upon a difference of opinion among the judges, ordered to be reargued, and after that only four of the seven judges concurred in the final judgment of the court. Thus five out of eleven judges sustained the view upon which Mr. Shaw originally commenced the suit. (See 11 Peters, 536.)

Between the times when the subject of this sketch argued his first modest five-dollar case and the above-named celebrated case, he was engaged in a wide and varied practice in the State courts. During the same period he often represented the town of Boston in the Legislature, and was a member when the first charter of the City of Boston was granted, and he was in fact the author of that charter.

He was a member of the house of Representatives when Judge Prescott was impeached for maladministration in his office of Judge of Probate. He was elected one of the seven managers, to represent the House in the trial of the impeachment before the Senate, and argued the cause for the prosecution in reply to Mr. Webster's argument for the defence. A competent judge of the comparative merits of the two arguments has said: "The argument of Mr. Shaw may be read immediately after that of Mr. Webster, without feeling that there is any descent. It has not the rhetoric of Mr. Webster, — eloquence, if that is a better word; but it is robust, manly sense, in clear and vigorous English. Its tone and temper are judicial, as became the speaker's position."

Besides performing his duties as a legislator with great ability and fidelity, he took an active part in the municipal affairs of the town, and repeatedly served as selectman and member of the school board. He was also one of the delegates from the town of Boston to the Constitutional Convention of 1820. He was one of the Commissioners appointed under a resolve of the Legislature to collect and edit the laws of the Commonwealth for publication, previous to the revision of 1836. He enriched the legal literature of the times by frequent contributions to the Law Magazines. In all these ways he employed his extraordinary natural endowments, and became both a profound jurist and wise man of affairs. He was intimately and thoroughly acquainted with the people and institutions of his own time, and it may with entire truthfulness be said of him, as he said of Chief Justice Parsons, that, " no person was probably more thoroughly versed in the early history, laws, institutions, manners, and local usages of the early settlers of New England; and the public are deeply indebted to him for much that has been preserved on these subjects in the reports of his judicial decisions."

Thus with a mind of great native force and comprehensiveness, furnished and disciplined in the highest and best possible manner, by study and practice, Lemuel Shaw, at the ripe age of fifty, without ever having before held a judicial office, was made Chief Justice of the Supreme Court of Massachusetts; and from the day he entered upon the discharge of the duties of that high office, until at the end of thirty years, still in the full possession of his mental powers, he voluntarily resigned its honors and duties, he enjoyed without interruption the profound respect and confidence of the Bar and people of the Commonwealth. This universal confidence in his judicial integrity and ability was gained and retained by a firm, fearless, intelligent, and impartial administration of justice, under the forms and in strict compliance with the rules of law; although the judgments he sometimes, as a judge, felt compelled to pronounce, subjected him to misconception and even temporary obloquy.

For while he paid due deference to an enlightened public sentiment, the passionate and unreasoning demands of popular clamor had no terrors for him, and could never silence in him the voice of conscience or the call to duty.

Rufus Choate, in his very eloquent and well-considered argument in the Constitutional Convention of 1853 in favor of an independent judiciary, while describing the qualities of a good judge, said : —

In the first place, he should be profoundly learned in all the learning of the law, and he must know how to use that learning. . . . He is to know . . . not constitutional and statute law alone, but that other ampler, that boundless jurisprudence, the common law brought by our ancestors from England, but which in the progress of centuries we have ameliorated, and enriched, and adapted wisely to the necessities of a busy, prosperous, and wealthy community. . . .

In the next place, he must be a man, not merely upright, . . . but a man who will not respect persons in judgment. . . . If, on one side, is the executive power, and the legislature and the people, — the sources of his honors, the givers of his daily bread, — and on the other an individual, nameless and odious, his eye is to see neither great nor small, — attending only to the " trepidations of the balance." If a law is passed by a unanimous legislature, clamored for by the general voice of the public, and a cause is before him on it, in which the whole community is on one side and an individual nameless or odious on the other, and he believes it to be against the Constitution, he must so declare it, — or there is no judge. . . .

And finally, he must possess the perfect confidence of the community, that he bear not the sword in vain. To be honest, to be no respecter of persons, is not yet enough. He must be believed such ; . . . he should be a man toward whom the love and trust and affectionate admiration of the people should flow ; not a man perching for a winter and summer in our court-houses, and then gone forever ; but one to whose benevolent face, and bland and dignified manners, and firm administration of the whole learning of the law, we become accustomed,

. . . toward whom our attachment and trust grow even with the growth of his own eminent reputation.

This was at the time believed to be no ideal picture sketched from the exhaustless resources of the great orator, but a correct delineation of the character of the eminent Chief Justice, whose great reputation probably contributed more than any other thing, to prevent the disastrous change in the constitution of the court over which he presided which was favored by a majority of the Convention, but was not ratified by the people.

Judge Shaw was a magistrate of inflexible firmness and dauntless moral courage. With the loftiest sense of natural justice, and the deepest abhorrence of all wrong and oppression, he nevertheless believed it to be his duty, as a judge, to pronounce judgments in all cases according to the established law of the land, however much such judgments might be in conflict with the passions and popular sentiment of the passing day. As soon would those who knew him well, expect to see the law of gravitation changed or suspended, to save some incautious victim from a falling tower beneath which he was passing, as that the Chief Justice would attempt, in a particular case, to work out some imaginary or real equity, but which could only be done by a false interpretation and violation of the law and Constitution he had sworn to uphold and support.

His distinguished successor in office, and who had been an Associate Justice in the same court many years, has left this testimony as to his intellectual and moral qualities : —

His greatness was the combined result of an intellect of the first order, cultivated and trained by a patient industry which never tired. He was endowed by nature with extraordinary powers; and yet they were in such just proportion and symmetry, the different faculties were so blended and harmonized, that it is difficult to designate any one which can be said to have constituted his distinguishing intellectual character. No subject was so great as to be beyond the reach of his comprehensive grasp; no distinction so nice or minute as to elude his keen and discriminating observation: . . . capable of dealing with abstract propositions, and of discussing principles and theories without reference to their practical application, no one could more readily adapt them to the daily business and concerns of life. With a simplicity of character and truthfulness almost childlike, he united a sagacity and clear insight into motives and actions of others, which enabled him to detect deceit and hypocrisy at a glance. Firm, courageous, and inflexible, he was also gentle, affectionate, and kind. But above all he had that clear and unerring judgment, that just perception of the right, that instinctive knowledge of the true relations of things, which may be best described as good, sound, Anglo-Saxon common-sense.

There is another important element of character, which should never be overlooked in any estimate of that of Chief Justice Shaw. Mr. Webster, speaking of his great contemporary and friend, Jeremiah Mason, after the death of the latter, said : " Mr. Mason's religious sentiments and feelings were the crowning glories of his character ; " and added : "*Religion* is a necessary and indispensable element in any great human character." It certainly pervaded and formed a permanent part of the character of Chief Justice Shaw. He ever maintained a devout and reverent spirit, habitually recognizing his dependence upon God. One of the first things he did, upon taking his seat for the first time upon the Bench, at the September term, 1830, in Berkshire County, was to deliver an address before the assembled Bar of that county, upon the life and character of his predecessor, Chief Justice Parker. Referring, at the close of his address, to the sudden death of Judge Parker, he said : —

May this inspire every mind with the importance of filling up life with usefulness ; and by constant benevolence to man, by humble and devout piety towards God, of being at all times prepared for a like instant departure from the labors and cares and anxieties of this transitory life, to the world of rest, of peace, and hope, beyond the grave.

Thirty years afterwards, in his reply to the address of the Bar of the Commonwealth upon the occasion of resigning his office, he used this impressive language : —

Gentlemen, in this slight retrospect of my judicial course, indeed in reviewing the whole course of my life, I desire in this solemn hour to express my sincere and devout gratitude to that benignant and overruling Providence who has crowned my days with innumerable blessings, without whose sustaining aid all human strength is but weakness, and the highest human exertions but vanity.

It cannot be regarded as irrelevant to this line of thought to notice, in passing, the remarkable coincidence in the history of human progress, that the great founders of modern science, and the great jurists and judges to whom we are indebted for the grandest systems of modern jurisprudence, were devout men. The founders of physical science, in their researches among second causes, never forgot the First Great Cause, as some of the more recent celebrities of science have done; nor did the great jurists, the founders of our jurisprudence, attempt to establish justice upon the uncertain and ever-shifting principles of a merely utilitarian philosophy, but rather upon the eternal and permanent distinctions between right and wrong, constituting the foundation of the moral law.

No adequate account can here be given of Judge Shaw's judicial labors, extending, as we have seen, through a period of thirty years, and embracing an almost endless variety of subjects. His opinions, if collected and published separately, would fill nearly or quite twenty volumes as large as the Massachusetts Reports; and it would not be difficult to compile from these opinions a treatise of rare excellence on nearly every branch of the law; for

Judge Shaw did not content himself with simply deciding the questions raised in the case, and citing authorities in support of his decisions, but by a process of original reasoning, both profound and comprehensive, reached his conclusions and vindicated their soundness. His definitions and expositions of the fundamental principles of law are as luminous and exact as the axioms and demonstrations in mathematics.

During his long term of office great and frequent changes were made in the laws, in the organization and jurisdiction of the courts, and in the forms of pleading and procedure. During the same period the great industrial interests of the State were multiplied a thousand-fold, and new and difficult questions thence arising were constantly presented for the consideration of the court, whose duty it became to adjust and adapt the established principles of law to an entirely new order of things. It was then that the railroad system had its beginning, and marvellously rapid development, displacing the earlier but less efficient means of travel and transportation, and bringing along with the change the inevitable legal problems for solution by the courts, as to how the new franchise could be granted and enjoyed without unjustly interfering with or destroying vested rights acquired under the old; and it was during this period, also, that the great manufacturing enterprises in this State, having been begun a few years before 1830 under the change of policy by the Federal government in relation to the tariff, demanded the constant attention and taxed the learning of the court to settle all their conflicting claims and rights on such broad and permanent principles that capital invested and labor employed in them could clearly understand by what rules of law they were to be protected and governed.

But with his view of the common law, as expressed in the following extract from his opinion in Common-

wealth *vs.* Temple, 14 Gray, it was less difficult to adapt
established principles of law to new exigencies as they
arose : —

It is the great merit of the common law that it is founded
upon a comparatively few broad general principles of justice,
fitness, and expediency, the correctness of which is generally
acknowledged, and which at first are few and simple, but which
carried out in their practical details, and adapted to extremely
complicated cases of fact, give rise to many and often perplexing
questions ; yet these original principles remain fixed, and are
generally comprehensive enough to adapt themselves to new institutions and conditions of society, new modes of commerce, new
usages and practices as the progress of society in the advancement of civilization may require.

The law of Massachusetts, as now perfectly well established, by which the rights of mill-owners and other ripa-
rian proprietors to water, as a means of power and for
other purposes, are determined and regulated, may be said
with almost literal accuracy to be the creation of Chief
Justice Shaw's judicial mind. His opinion in the case of
Cary *vs.* Daniels, 8 Metcalf, is a condensed statement of
the whole law on the subject. It is a piece of pure juridi-
cal reasoning from beginning to end. No authorities are
cited, and none are needed; it is its own great authority. The flow of the argument is clear as a crystal stream
from the mountain, and every sentence is luminous with
its own light.

In a series of opinions given by the Chief Justice on
the subject of taking private property for public uses,
under the right of eminent domain, all the principles of
that most important branch of the law are elaborately
discussed, and its distinctions and qualifications clearly
stated. In Commonwealth *vs.* Tewksbury, 11 Metcalf, he
discusses the distinction between taking property for public use and restraining the owner from making use of his
property to the injury of another or to the public detri-

ment. In that case the defendant claimed that a penal statute which forbid his removing stones, gravel, and sand from a beach owned by him was unconstitutional, as it provided no reasonable compensation to him for thus depriving him of such use of his property as he chose to make of it; but he learned at the end of his controversy with the government that "all property is acquired and held under the tacit condition that it shall not be so used as to injure the equal rights of others, or to delay, stay, or greatly impair the public rights and interests of the community." The Chief Justice in this case, with his accustomed penetration, strikes down to the primal principles on which all property rights rest, and shows that the condition was not something superadded by the government to the estate after its acquisition by the owner, but that it was inherent in the original title; and therefore the government, by depriving the owner of the forbidden use of his property, took nothing from him for which he was entitled to compensation. In another series of decisions the Chief Justice expounds with great learning and historical research the rights of land-owners whose estates border on the seashore. In these cases he shows his entire familiarity with the early history of the colonies and their legislation. In an article published in the American Jurist of January, 1829, he discussed some of the aspects of this subject, successfully controverting the opinion expressed by Chief Justice Parsons in Storer *vs.* Freeman, 6 Massachusetts, to the effect that the vacating of the colony charter annulled the laws and ordinances passed under it, and showing that the opinion was erroneous. In another series of cases the whole system of what may be called the railroad law of Massachusetts, so far as that depends upon judicial decisions, was developed and formulated. But we can enter upon no analysis of these cases here.

Since undertaking this sketch the writer has re-examined every one of Chief Justice Shaw's opinions on questions of constitutional law, arising under either the State Constitution or that of the United States; and it seems to be hazarding but little to say that no judge of any court was ever called upon to decide a greater number or variety of this class of important causes; and that no judge, with perhaps the single exception of Chief Justice Marshall, ever discussed these questions with a greater wealth of learning, with a more comprehensive view of the whole field of debate, or with a more profound insight into the nature and structure of our complex system of government. No better statement of the subject can be found anywhere than in his opinion in the case of Commonwealth *vs.* Kimball, 24 Pickering, where he says:—

The great and leading object of this complex system of government was to select a few great and important subjects of administration, in which all the States, and the people of all the States, had a common interest, to confide them to the general government, with all the collateral, incidental, and implied powers and functions necessary to a full and entire performance of all the duties of such a government. All other powers of sovereign government, necessary or proper to provide for the peace, safety, health, morals, and general welfare of the community, remain entire and uncontrolled to the State government.

And in the same case he declares, as a leading canon of construction, that —

In considering the Constitution and laws of the United States and those of the several States, and deciding whether their respective provisions do come in conflict or not, and to what extent, it is proper and absolutely necessary to have a just regard to the laws and institutions of the country and of the respective States as they existed before the formation and adoption of the Constitution of the United States, and to the objects and purposes had in view by that Constitution.

And in Commonwealth *vs.* Blackington, 24 Pickering, he says:—

In construing the Constitution of this State, it must never be forgotten that it was not intended to contain a detailed system of practical rules for the regulation of the government in after times; but that it was rather intended, after an organization of the government, and distributing the executive, legislative, and judicial powers amongst its several departments, to declare a few broad, general, fundamental principles for their guidance and general direction.

Whoever reads Judge Shaw's opinions on constitutional law will not be likely to read them aright unless he constantly bears in mind these, his cardinal rules of interpretation and construction. The candid and careful reader of his decision in the Syms case, 7 Cushing, will find that that decision is based mainly upon the historical argument, — an argument which it is far more easy passionately to condemn than to answer; and whoever will read his opinion in Commonwealth *vs.* Aves, 18 Pickering, and his powerful discussion of the Missouri question, in an article published in the North American Review, January, 1820, will not for a moment believe that his opinion in the Syms case was the result of any want of the deepest detestation of the institution of slavery or condemnation of it as the entire subversion of every dictate and right of natural justice.

His opinion in Commonwealth *vs.* Anthes, 5 Gray, as to the respective rights and duties of juries and the court in the trial of criminal cases, notwithstanding the brilliant dissenting opinion delivered by Judge Thomas in that case, has become the settled law of the Commonwealth; and the result is, we have in this respect " a government of laws and not of men; " and the right of trial by jury in this Commonwealth is to-day more secure and of higher value by reason of the great argument of the Chief Justice in its support in the case of Jones *vs.* Robbins, 8 Gray, than it would have been had the dissenting opinion in that case become the established law. And although the

Supreme Court of the United States, in a recent decision, in Hartado *vs.* People of California, 110 Otto, has given to the phrase, "due process of law," or law of the land, a construction different from that maintained by Judge Shaw in Jones *vs.* Robbins, and so apparently overruling the decision of our court so far as to hold that an information may take the place of an indictment in a criminal prosecution; yet that does not materially impair the great value of the opinion of the Chief Justice as a defence of this great safeguard of life and liberty, the trial by jury; besides the circumstances under which the two cases came before the courts were quite unlike. In the latter case, Jones had been tried upon a *complaint*, in a police court, of an offence which would subject him to an "infamous punishment;" and in the opinion of Chief Justice Shaw, the act of the Legislature which authorized such trial before a police court without a jury, and even without an information, was void as being in violation of the twelfth article of the Declaration of Rights. In the case of Hartado *vs.* California, the Federal court held that the words "due process of law," in the fourteenth amendment of the Constitution of the United States, do not necessarily require an indictment by a grand jury in a prosecution for murder. How far this decision was affected by the fact that the Constitution of California authorizes prosecutions for felonies by information, *after* examination and commitment by a magistrate, without an indictment by a grand jury, does not appear; and it is very certain that the opinion of Mr. Justice Matthews in the California case has by the force of its reasoning given no additional strength to the very able dissenting opinion of Justice Merrick in the Massachusetts case. It should be said, in this connection, that Mr. Justice Harlan did not concur in the judgment of the court in the former case, and delivered an able dissenting opinion, sustaining the views of our State court; and no sound or sufficient reason has yet been shown for a new interpretation of the "nisi per legem terræ" of Magna Charta, or our own Bill of Rights; nor any reason why the safeguards and immunities thrown around those charged with high crimes, and prosecuted with all the force of government, should be broken down or weakened.

In another important criminal cause, the judgment of the court, delivered by the Chief Justice, encountered the dissenting opinion of his venerable Associate, Mr. Justice Wilde. The case referred to is Commonwealth *vs.* York, 9 Met. The defendant was indicted for the murder of one Norton. There was plenary evidence that the defendant inflicted upon the deceased a mortal wound with a dirk-knife, which penetrated the heart. There was an attempt at the trial to show the offence was only manslaughter. The court instructed the jury upon this part of the case, that "the rule of law is, when the fact of killing is proved to have been committed by the accused, *and nothing further is shown*, the presumption of law is that it is malicious, and an act of murder. It follows, therefore, that in such cases the proof of matter of excuse or extenuation lies on the accused; and this may appear either from evidence adduced by the prosecution, or evidence offered by the defendant." This instruction was claimed by the defendant's counsel to be erroneous, and was made the basis of a motion for a new trial; and it was upon this motion that the judgment of the court and the dissenting opinion were given. The rule of law laid down by the court was claimed to be erroneous, because, as was said by the defendant's counsel, it cast upon the defendant the burden of *disproving* malice, which is an essential element of murder, and it is the duty of the prosecution to prove every part of the offence beyond a reasonable doubt. The fallacy of the counsel's argument and of the dissenting opinion arises entirely from a misinterpretation of the instructions given to the jury. The court nowhere intimates that the burden is not upon the prosecution to make out every part of the case, by proof of the guilt of the defendant beyond every reasonable doubt. On the contrary, the court assumes that to be the rule, and that the burden of proof upon the issue of guilt or innocence never changes. What the court says, and what the Chief Justice in his very thorough discussion of the subject insists upon, is, that if the fact of killing is clearly proved, and nothing else appears, — no explanation, no qualification, of the act is shown, either by the defendant or in the evidence of the prosecution, — that in itself proves the killing to have been malicious. But if the accused sets up in his defence matter of excuse or extenuation, as that the killing was accidental, in self-defence, or in the heat of blood, the burden of proof upon the issue thus raised is upon him. A careful study of this opinion of the Chief Justice will show that it is supported both by reason and authority. At the close of the opinion he says: "The crime, the *corpus delicti*, is to be proved beyond reasonable doubt, otherwise the accused is entitled to an acquittal. The jury must be so instructed, and were so instructed in the present case. If the homicide was proved beyond reasonable doubt, and no fact of extenuation came out with the proof of the homicide, then the offence of which the party was convicted was proved beyond reasonable doubt; and the doubt arises only in regard to a fact which was alleged by the accused in extenuation, but not proved." This is and has been the law, not only in cases of homicide, but in every other species of criminal prosecution. The principles laid down in the York case were applied by the Chief Justice in the more celebrated Webster trial, and for this he at the time received, from some not well-informed sources, a measure of unfriendly and unjust but harmless criticism.

It would be a grateful task to follow the footsteps of the great Chief Justice farther along the heights of our

ever expanding jurisprudence, and to note his large and
liberal contributions to this proud and noble system of
law, developed under free institutions, by and for a free
and intelligent people. It is said by the incomparable
historian of the Decline and Fall of the Roman Empire,
that "the laws of a nation constitute the most important
part of its history;" and that part of history, it may
truly be said, is not made by warriors, diplomatists, or
politicians, but by the great jurists of the nation who
preside over its courts, and by their writings give form
and character to its jurisprudence.

But this sketch, necessarily brief, would be altogether
too incomplete if closed without stating the fact that Judge
Shaw was quite as well qualified to preside at a nisi prius
term as at the head of the full court sitting as a law court,
and that he was all the better fitted for the latter duty by
reason of his familiarity with the former. One of his most
accomplished Associates during the last years of his judicial
life has said : —

The province of a judge is to find and apply to the varied
exigencies of life and business, not an abstract, but the practical, working rule. The skill, discretion, and tact requisite to
do this well are the fruit of business training got either upon
the bench or before one gets there. Hence it is that some labor
at nisi prius — the putting the rules of law into harness, and
seeing just how they will draw — seems to be indispensable, not
merely to the making, but to the preservation of a good judge.
A court without experience in trials gets to be practically, as
well as technically, a court of *errors*.

At the time Judge Shaw first took his seat on the bench
of the Supreme Court, that court had, besides its original
jurisdiction, a large appellate jurisdiction in both civil and
criminal causes. This appellate jurisdiction in criminal
matters was abolished in 1839, and that in civil matters
in 1840 ; but the nisi prius business in the Supreme Court

continued to a very considerable extent so long as Judge Shaw remained at the head of that court.

The equity jurisdiction of the court, very limited at first, was, during the thirty years of Judge Shaw's service on the bench, enlarged from time to time, by acts of the Legislature; though the act granting full equity jurisdiction to the court was not passed until 1857, only three years before the resignation of the Chief Justice. All prior acts contained grants of specific and limited equity powers, thus increasing the difficulty of the task imposed upon the court, of establishing rules and a system of practice that should not be in conflict with the statutes, and at the same time should be, to the extent of the jurisdiction granted, in harmony with the general principles of chancery practice. But no one knew better than the Chief Justice did that the fundamental principles of law and equity are the same ; and with his thorough mastery of those principles, he followed without difficulty and met every new demand arising from the progress made by legislation in this most important jurisdiction, both in its theories and practice ; and when the judicial history of Massachusetts shall be fully written, and doing full justice to his very learned and able associates, it will still appear that Chief Justice Shaw, in this department of the law as well as in every other, did more than any other man of his time to render life, liberty, property, and reputation secure in the Commonwealth that trusted him with her highest honors for nearly a third of a century, and whose honor was ever safe in his keeping.

CHIEF JUSTICE SHAW

By HON. BENJAMIN F. THOMAS, LL.D.

BE it book, essay, judicial opinion, or legal argument, we read it with more interest — nay, with better understanding — if we know something of the writer, of his culture, manners, and way of life. To be told even when and where he was born, lived, and died, serves as an introduction: we feel more at our ease with him. To study, criticise, and inwardly digest the opinions of eminent judges, is a large part of the work of a lawyer's life. Analysis and logic are, indeed, no great respecters of persons, and, where the reasons of the judgment are given, will probe and test them. But moral reasoning, with which jurisprudence has to do, is perhaps never thoroughly impersonal, never wholly free from the quality of the thinker and writer. Sometimes, too, we get the decision of the judge without the reasons which led to it; and then we must weigh the judge. The reporter tells us, "the Lord Chancellor held;" and we know the Chancellor was Lord Hardwicke.

To the students of the law (we are all students), to our younger brothers of the profession, the lives of great judges and lawyers, however imperfectly told, may reveal the paths to the heights of professional excellence, and show how its fields of conflict and trial are won, — may assure them that no life is more thoroughly devoted to the service of one's country and of mankind, than that which is given to the just administration of the laws, and to make them wiser and better.

It was part, therefore, of our plan, to give to our readers, by way of review, memoirs and notices of eminent judges and lawyers, especially of our own country, where biographies have been given to the public; and when no memoir has been published, by supplying, as far as practicable and our limits would permit, the deficiency. The latter is the case with the eminent jurist who was for thirty years Chief Justice of Massachusetts. He died in the spring of 1861, just at the outbreak of the great rebellion. Though the Bar of the State and its courts united in tributes of respect and veneration to his memory, and arrangements were made for the delivery of a eulogy at a future day, the person selected for the duty being for some time withdrawn into the public service, and the profession, as well as the public at large, absorbed in the interests and duties and passions of the great conflict, the duty was never performed. If this sketch should help even to supply the deficiency, the writer will be content. The reader will not look for stirring incident in judicial life, or in the preparation. Some idea of the culture and discipline by which the great magistrate was built up, possibly may be got; by that considerable class who console themselves with the thought, that " they also serve who only stand and wait," some solace and encouragement.

Lemuel Shaw was born in Barnstable, Massachusetts, on the 9th of January, 1781, within three months from the time when the Constitution and frame of government, under which his life was to be spent and which his judicial labors were to illustrate, went into operation. Within the year of his birth was won the great victory which secured the independence of his country. His father and grandfather were clergymen. His grandfather, John Shaw, the minister of Bridgewater, educated four sons at Harvard College, all of whom became Congregational ministers.

Of these, the Rev. Oakes Shaw, the father of the Chief Justice, was settled in the West Parish in Barnstable, in 1760, and continued in the pastorate till his death in 1807. That he was faithful to his people, and that they loved and honored him, this long connection would show; though we are not to forget that pastors were not then settled on horseback with a view to early removal, and that " Providence " did not then so often call rising young ministers from small rural parishes to opulent city ones.

The son always spoke of his father with the highest veneration and respect; never without emotion. At the centennial celebration at Barnstable in 1839, more than thirty years after his father's death, he thus touched upon a subject always near to his heart: —

Almost within sight of the place where we are, still stands a modest spire, marking the spot where a beloved father stood to minister the holy word of truth and hope and salvation to a numerous, beloved, and attached people, for almost half a century. Pious, pure, simple-hearted, devoted to and beloved by his people, never shall I cease to venerate his memory, or to love those who knew and loved him. I speak in the presence of some who knew him, and of many more who, I doubt not, were taught to love and honor his memory, as one of the earliest lessons of their childhood.

The mother of the Chief Justice was Susannah Hayward, of Braintree. She was the sister of Dr. Lemuel Hayward, an eminent physician of Boston, from whom her son was named. The mother was a woman of vigorous powers, mental and physical. She lived to see and enjoy the success and honors of her son; dying under his roof in 1839, at the extreme age of ninety-four. How much of our history is crowded into that life, — the "Seven Years' War;" the War of Separation and Independence; the struggle for national unity, for commercial freedom; the birth and maturing to manhood of a great nation.

Lemuel was fitted for college in part by his father, and
partly at Braintree. In 1796, at the age of fifteen, he
entered the Freshman Class at Cambridge. During the
winter vacations of the last three years, to help pay the
college bills and to relieve his father, he kept a district
school. In the way of discipline and preparation for active life, we doubt not those winter vacations were worth
more than any part of the college course. Indeed, no
man thoroughly understands New England life and manners who has not kept a district school and " boarded
round."

The Class of 1800 had in it three, at least, marked
men: Washington Allston, the painter-poet; the eloquent and saintly Buckminster; and Lemuel Shaw.
Other eminent men were President Bates, of Middlebury
College; Rev. Dr. Lowell; and Timothy Flint, whose
letters from the valley of the Mississippi charmed every-
body, forty years ago. Lemuel held a good rank in his
class, and, at Commencement, took part in a Greek dialogue with Timothy Flint. The Hebrew orator has
escaped our memory.

After leaving college, Lemuel was, for a year, usher
in the Franklin, now Brimmer, School, in Boston. During the same year, he was a writer, or assistant editor,
for the Boston Gazette. The Gazette was a most ardent supporter of the Federal party and politics. At
this time the paper also had a literary character, with
several able contributors, — Robert Treat Paine, jun.,
author of Adams and Liberty, who wrote the dramatic
articles and criticisms; Thomas O. Selfridge, soon to ac-
quire so unhappy a distinction; David Everett, then at
the Bar, but afterwards first editor of the Boston Pa-
triot; and, above all, Fisher Ames.

At the end of the year, he commenced the study of the
law with David Everett. Mr. Everett was a scholar and
writer; wrote Phi Beta poems, dramas, essays, political

and literary; and on the fulfilment of the Prophecies, in which he assumes to prove, that the United States were distinctly alluded to by Daniel and St. John; and, more than all, the wonderful poem, —

> " You 'd scarce expect one of my age
> To speak in public on the stage."

Mr. Everett removed from Boston to Amherst, New Hampshire; and his student, Mr. Shaw, went with him, and there completed his term of study. Mr. Everett, who had been at the Bar but two or three years when Lemuel entered his office, seems to have devoted himself to almost everything but the law. He soon after left the profession for more congenial pursuits, though not more successful.

With what diligence Mr. Shaw pursued his studies under Mr. Everett, we cannot affirm; but, either then or at a later period, he must have studied the law, as a science, carefully and thoroughly. He had that familiarity with and wide comprehension of the principles of the law, and that facility and ease in their application, which come from patient and systematic study, and are seldom or never the result of practice only, — of cramming for the emergency.

Mr. Shaw was admitted to the Bar of New Hampshire, in September, 1804, and, in the following October, at a term of the Supreme Court at Plymouth, as an attorney in this Commonwealth. So great have been the legal products of New Hampshire, and her contributions to the Bar of Massachusetts (Webster, Mason, Fletcher, Parker), and so large our debt, that we cannot afford to give her any credit for Lemuel Shaw. He was but a pilgrim and sojourner in that cradle-land of great lawyers.

The cases decided at the October term of Plymouth and Barnstable, 1804, are found in the first volume of the Massachusetts Reports. So that the professional life of Mr. Shaw begins with the system by which con-

sistency, harmony, and symmetry were to be given to
the then shapeless mass of our common law, — the work
to which his labors were so largely to contribute.

Mr. Shaw settled in Boston. He had an office in the
old State House with Thomas O. Selfridge. Whether
there was a partnership, we do not understand. He testified at the trial, that he had an office with him. And
that was his expression to the writer. After his trial
and acquittal, Mr. Selfridge removed to New York, and
the connection, if there was any, was dissolved.

Mr. Shaw did not find his way readily to large practice,
or rise rapidly to distinction. But this was very far from
being a misfortune. An early plunge into business would
have made him a ready man; but time and opportunity
for study, wisely improved, made him a full one. The
qualities that readily attract business do not always secure and retain it. If Mr. Shaw's progress was slow,
every step was on solid ground. There was no slumping,
no falling back. If he had work to do, he did it as well
and thoroughly as he could, and thus prepared himself to
do the next better.

The first case in which his name appears in the reports,
is Young vs. Adams, 6 Mass. 162 (1810). The amount involved was five dollars. The case was this: A note was
payable in foreign bills. The promisor paid it, and the
note was given up; but one of the bills given in payment was a counterfeit bill. The payee brought his action for the amount of the counterfeit note. Mr. Shaw
put his defence on two grounds: first, that an action for
money had and received would not lie; and, secondly
(the ground on which he principally relied), that where
there was no fraud and no express undertaking, and both
the parties were equally innocent, no action would lie.
The court, by Mr. Justice Sewall, said " the two questions
had been fully and ingeniously argued" by defendant's
counsel, and, we hardly need to add, decided for the

plaintiff. This was a small beginning; but perhaps the future Chief Justice recalled the encouraging lines of Master Everett, —

" Large streams from little fountains flow;
Tall oaks from little acorns grow."

Mr Shaw was in practice twenty-six years. He devoted himself faithfully to the study and work of his profession, but not to the utter exclusion of other studies. A man cannot be a great lawyer who is nothing else. Exclusive devotion to the study and practice of the law tends to acumen rather than breadth, to subtlety rather than strength. The air is thin among the apices of the law, as on the granite needles of the Alps. Men must find refreshment and strength in the quiet valleys at their feet. For the comprehensive grasp of principles, for the faculty of applying and illustrating them; for the power to reach just conclusions, and to lead other minds to them, breadth of culture is necessary. Some other things are to be studied beside the reports and text-books.

The law is not " a jealous mistress; " she is a very sensible mistress. She expects you to keep regular hours; but an evening with the Muses or the Graces does not awake her ire.

The mind requires not only diversity of discipline, but generosity of diet. It cannot grow to full, well-rounded proportions, on any one aliment. Mr. Shaw understood this, and read and studied and observed much outside of Coke and Blackstone.

He did not, we think, keep up his intimacy with the Greek and Latin. He could not have written a Greek dialogue as well at fifty as at nineteen. But he was at home with the English classics, and a master of the English tongue. He liked the elder English novelists and satirists, — Swift, De Foe, Fielding, and Smollett.

He was a student and admirer of Hogarth, and used to call our attention to minute details of his pictures, showing the artist's nice touch and the student's careful eye.

He was a close observer of Nature, — of the trees of the forest, and of the wild-flowers and their haunts. He had a strong taste and love of mechanics and of the mechanic arts. A new machine was a delight to him, and after court he must go down to the machine-shop or manufactory to see it in operation.

He took great interest in the affairs of the town, the then town, of Boston; was fire warden, school committeeman, Fourth of July orator, and for several years one of the selectmen.

He had a strong interest in the affairs of the State; was for eight years a Representative from the town of Boston in the General Court; and for three or four years Senator from Suffolk.

He was an ardent Federalist, and a firm supporter of the Federal Policy, State and national, from the beginning of the century to the dissolution of the party; and, what is to his credit, he never apologized for it in public or private. But he had too catholic a spirit for a mere partisan. He was a working member of the Legislature, giving his time to the service of the Commonwealth in useful and practical legislation. We know of no training and experience for the young lawyer better than two or three winters in a State Legislature; provided he goes there to study and to work, and not merely to dabble in party politics or make high-falutin speeches.

Of the practical and useful character of his work, one or two illustrations may be given. While a member of the Senate, he was chairman of the joint committee to whom was referred the petition for a city charter for the town of Boston. He drew up the charter and plan of city government. This was then a new work, and required not only familiarity with the working of our town governments, but foresight and constructive skill. The work was well done, and eminently successful in practical operation. Mr. Shaw took always a deep interest in the working of the new system of government, and in the general progress and welfare of the city.[1] While a member of the House, Mr. Shaw was appointed one of the commissioners to publish a new and revised edition of the General Laws of the Commonwealth. His associate in the commission was Professor Asahel Stearns, of Cambridge. How thoroughly well and faithfully this work was done, the older members of the profession have reason to gratefully recollect. This was the edition in exclusive use from 1820 to the general revision of the Statutes in 1836, and is still indispensable for reference.

These details may, we fear, be uninteresting; but the labors of Mr. Shaw as school committee-man, selectman, representative, in editing the Statutes and framing the city charter, make up part of the discipline, training, and experience of the great magistrate. He obviously is not the great judge who has studied law only as a science and in the books, but who has seen and known how it works in the daily business of life. The province of the judge is to find and apply to the varied exigencies of life and business, not an abstract, but the practical, working rule. The skill and discretion and tact requisite to do this well, are the fruit of business training, got either upon the bench or before one gets there. Hence it is that some work at *nisi prius*, — the putting the rules of law to work, and seeing just how they work, seems to be indispensable, not merely to the making, but to the preservation, of a good judge. A court without experience

---

[1] He was, in a sense, *conditor urbis*. His large services to the city and to the Commonwealth, of which the city is the head, fairly claim some memorial of her respect and gratitude. Would it not be a graceful thing for the city to place a duplicate of Hunt's great picture of the Chief Justice in Faneuil Hall?

in trials, gets to be practically, as well as technically, a
" court of errors."

In the Convention of 1820, to revise the Constitution
of the State, Mr. Shaw was a delegate from the town of
Boston.

The separation of the District of Maine from Massachusetts, and its admission into the Union as an independent
State, seemed to render such revision necessary. The
Convention was unquestionably the ablest body of men
that ever assembled in the Commonwealth. It was in
constant session some eight weeks. The old Constitution
had been adopted in the midst of the Revolution, and
had been in operation for forty years. It is marvellous
to see how slight the changes that were made: so wisely
and firmly had the men of 1781 builded, that little modi-
fication or repair of their structure was required. It re-
flects the highest honor upon the men of 1781 that their
work needed so little change ; and upon the men of 1820
that they had the sense to see it, and to let well enough
alone. Some tolerably sensible men think that most of
the changes since adopted are proof also of the wise for-
bearance of the Convention of 1820.

The fact is, that even the Convention of 1781 had but
few structural changes to make, when the Province of
Massachusetts Bay became an independent Commonwealth. There was the agony of birth and separation;
but the child was fully grown. States do *grow ;* they are
not *built up* with hammer and trowel, much less with " the
stuff that dreams are made of."

Mr. Shaw took a less active part in the labors and de-
bates of the Convention, than we should have anticipated
from his fitness for such work. When he addressed the
Convention it was upon practical subjects, — briefly, for-
cibly, and to the point. He spoke against a proposed
amendment, to make the stockholders of banks person-
ally liable ; in favor of the amendment giving authority

to the Legislature to establish city governments; in favor of an amendment requiring a vote of two-thirds of each branch of the Legislature to remove a judge from office by address; against an amendment of the Bill of Rights, which should give to a prisoner a right to be heard both by himself and counsel,—a right, by the way, which has always been practically enjoyed by prisoners, and which we have never known our courts to refuse.

It was while Mr. Shaw was a member of the House of Representatives of 1820–1821, that the impeachment and trial of Judge Prescott took place. An admirable report of this trial was made by two then young but accomplished members of the Bar. The trial, before the Senate of the Commonwealth, excited great attention, and was conducted with eminent ability on both sides. Judge Prescott was defended by an array of talent seldom enlisted in any cause, — Webster, Prescott, Blake, Hoar, Hubbard. The House had many eminent lawyers among its members, and King, Lincoln, Baylies, Dutton, Fay, Shaw, and Leland were elected managers. The judge was impeached for maladministration in his office of Judge of Probate, by the taking of illegal fees. Mr. Shaw was engaged throughout the trial, and argued the cause for the prosecution, in immediate reply to Mr. Webster's argument for the defence. The argument of Mr. Webster is among his collected works, and is familiar to the profession and to general readers. Mr. Webster had conducted the defence with great vigor, but defiantly, and with less discretion than marked his later efforts. The close of Mr. Webster's address has been often cited and recited, as a happy specimen of his eloquence. It made an impression upon the Senate: it would have made a deeper one upon a jury. We think the argument of Mr. Shaw may be read immediately after that of Mr. Webster, without feeling that there is any descent. It has not the rhetoric of Mr. Webster ; eloquence, if that is the better

word; but it is robust, manly sense, in clear, vigorous
English. Its tone and temper are somewhat judicial, as
became the speaker's position. As this is, we believe, the
only well-reported argument of Mr. Shaw while at the
Bar, we are tempted to cite a short passage at the opening, and a few sentences at the close, to show his style
and manner: —

Mr. PRESIDENT, — In common with the honorable managers
with whom I am associated, I trust that I am sufficiently impressed with the magnitude and importance of the transaction
in which we are now engaged. I am well aware of the dignity
of the high tribunal before which I stand ; of the duty of the
constitutional accusers, by whom this prosecution is instituted ;
of the elevated personal and official character of the accused ;
of the nature of the offences imputed to him ; and the deep and
intense interest which is felt by the community in the result of
this trial. It is perhaps true, that these transactions may be re-
corded and remembered ; that the principles advanced, and the
decisions made in the course of this trial, will continue to exert
an influence on society, either salutary or pernicious, long after
all those of us who, either as judges or as actors, have a share in
these proceedings, shall be slumbering with our fathers. And
yet I do not know that these considerations, serious and affect-
ing as they certainly are, can afford any precise or practical rule,
either for the conduct or decision of this cause. In questions of
policy and expediency, there is a latitude of choice ; and the
same end may be pursued by different means. But in the administration of justice, in questions of judicial controversy, there
can be but one right rule. Whether, therefore, the parties are
high or low ; whether the subject in controversy be of great or
of little importance, — the same principles of law, the same
rules of evidence, the same regard to rigid and exact justice,
must guide and govern the decision. ' Thou shalt do no un-
righteousness in judgment ; thou shalt not respect the person of
the poor, nor honor the person of the mighty ; but in righteousness shalt thou judge thy neighbor,' — is an injunction delivered
upon the highest authority, and enforced by the most solemn of
all sanctions.

Nor am I aware that powerful and animated appeals to your

compassion or resentment can have any considerable or lasting influence; they may, indeed, afford opportunity for the display of genius and eloquence, excite a momentary feeling of sympathy and admiration, and awake and command attention. Beyond this their influence would be pernicious and deplorable. If the charges brought against the respondent are satisfactorily proved, justice — that justice due to the violated rights of an injured community, that justice deserved by the breach of the most sacred obligations — demands a conviction from which no considerations of compassion can or ought to shield him. On the contrary, if these charges are not substantiated, or do not import criminality, no feelings of resentment, no prepossessions of guilt, however thoroughly impressed, can prevent his acquittal.

Mr. Shaw thus closed his address : —

Notwithstanding the length to which these remarks have extended, I am sensible that I have taken but an imperfect view of the details of this long and complicated case. But I address myself to experienced men, to intelligent judges, capable of estimating the qualities of conduct, and appreciating the force of evidence. We have no earnest invocation to make to the Judges of this honorable court, except that they will examine the case now submitted to them without fear, favor, affection, prejudice, or partiality; and pronounce their decision, not according to the momentary impulses of sympathy and compassion, but upon the invariable dictates of judgment and reason. If sensibility should usurp the seat of justice, and take the place of the understanding and judgment, laws would be unavailing, and all civil and social rights become fluctuating and uncertain. Justice might throw away her balance, for it would be useless; and her sword, for it would be mischievous. If punishment and disgrace are to overtake the respondent, it is because punishment and disgrace are the natural, the necessary, and the inevitable consequences of turpitude and crime. The representatives of the people of this Commonwealth demand at your hands no sacrifice of innocence: they ask for no victim to their resentment, for they have none to gratify. If, applying the evidence to the law in this case, this court can, consistently with the conclusions of enlightened and inflexible judgment, pronounce the respondent innocent, these representatives will rejoice to find that the reputation of this Commonwealth still remains pure and unspotted. But if their conclusions should be otherwise; if this court is satisfied that the respondent has abused the powers entrusted to him, disregarded the rights of others, and violated his high official duties, — the representatives of the people do earnestly hope, and confidently trust, that this high court, disregarding all consequences personal to the respondent, will pronounce such judgment on his conduct as will prove a salutary example to all others in authority, vindicate the honor and secure the rights of this Commonwealth, and enable them to transmit to posterity that unblemished reputation for purity, honesty, and integrity in the administration of justice, which has hitherto been the ornament and glory of Massachusetts.

Mr. Shaw, as before observed, was in practice twenty-six years. He occasionally went into the other counties, but his business was chiefly confined to the Boston courts. He worked alone, with brief exception, for the first sixteen years, and then took into partnership Mr. Sydney Bartlett, who had been his student, and who is now so well known to the Bar of the Commonwealth and in the Supreme Court at Washington.

Mr. Shaw travelled but little, was fond of home, but enjoyed greatly the meetings of the clubs of which he was a member, and other social gatherings. Pleasure was given as well as received. He had fine social qualities, large conversational powers, and a fund of good humor and quiet mirth.

He was twice married. His first marriage, at the somewhat mature age of thirty-seven, was with Eliza, a daughter of Josiah Knapp, Esq., a merchant of Boston. By her he had two children, — a son and daughter. His second marriage was in 1827, with Hope, a daughter of Dr. Samuel Savage, of Barnstable, by whom he had two sons, Lemuel and Samuel, both members of the Bar in Boston. Home was always a happy place to him; and he never was more attractive and delightful than at his own fireside.

Though he kept up his interest in public affairs, and was willing to go to the Legislature, he refused to go to Congress.

He wrote occasionally for the press, but on legal or constitutional questions. The article, for example, in the North American Review for January, 1820, on "Slavery and the Mission Question," which attracted much attention at the time, was from his pen. This article is an able exposition of the baneful character and effects of slavery, social and political; resists its further progress; insists upon making, as a condition of the admission of Missouri, the provision that slavery shall for ever be prohibited within it; and argues at length and with great ability that such a condition would have the force of compact, from which the State, after its admission, could not absolve itself. The convictions then expressed as to the influence of slavery, social, economical, and political, and the duty of the North to oppose and resist its extension, were, we have reason to believe, never modified.

He also wrote an article in the American Jurist of January, 1829, in which he criticises and shows the unsoundness of the doctrine (a nod of Homer) stated by Chief Justice Parsons, in Storer vs. Freeman, 6 Mass. 438, that the colony laws and ordinances were annulled with the charter under the authority of which they were made.

In this quarter of a century at the Bar, Mr. Shaw built up a solid professional reputation, and acquired a valuable practice; not a great many cases, but important and leading causes, like Charles River Bridge vs. Warren Bridge (7 Pick. 144), and Blake vs. Williams (6 Pick. 286), requiring hard work and tough conflict. His examinations and arguments of legal questions were comprehensive and thorough, not neglecting the precedents, but getting down always to the principles which underlie them. His addresses to the jury (we speak from reputation) were forcible, earnest, logical; not brief; with little rhetoric, but that good in quality.

Upon the death of Chief Justice Parker, in the summer of 1830, Mr. Shaw was appointed by Governor Lincoln (still surviving in a green and honored old age) his successor. The selection proved so wise and judicious, and reflected so much honor upon the Commonwealth, that one and another excellent gentleman has convinced himself that it was by his suggestion, and through his influence, that the appointment was made. But no man better understood the wants of the place than Governor Lincoln, or who was able to fill it. He had practised under the great Chief Justices, Parsons, Sewall, and Parker, and well understood that only a strong man could continue the line. He had been in both branches of the Legislature, in the Constitutional Convention, and on the Bench of the Supreme Court, and knew all the leading members of the Bar of the State. Mr. Shaw had been associated with him as counsel; had been with him in the Legislature, in the Convention; and had practised before him as judge. The idea that any person could find out some excellent lawyer, little known to the Executive (who had been himself on the Bench), and get him appointed Chief Justice of the Supreme Court, is simply absurd. The selection was made by Governor Lincoln, and is but one of many claims of this excellent magistrate to the respect and esteem of the Commonwealth.

It is true, however, that Mr. Shaw was unwilling at first to take the office; and a heavy pressure was brought to bear upon him before he consented to accept. He was then in the fiftieth year of his age, had won his way rather slowly, but surely, to eminent rank at the Bar, and to a valuable business. He had acquired a moderate property, and was living happily and to his taste. He had a growing family to support and educate. He knew a great place was to be filled, and was distrustful of himself. He felt that he ought to and must decline. In this exigency, Mr. Webster was requested by the Governor to confer with him, and urge his acceptance of the place.

Mr. Webster used to give a pleasant account of this conference. He found the future Chief Justice smoking his evening cigar. Mr. Webster could not join him. It was a weakness of this otherwise notable man, that he could not smoke. So Mr. Webster talked while Mr. Shaw smoked. Mr. Webster made a regular onslaught upon him. Conceding the personal and pecuniary sacrifice, he pressed upon him, with the greater earnestness, the public want and demand, the dignity and importance of the office, and the opportunity it presented of winning an honored name, by valuable and enduring service to the State. Mr. Shaw was silent, showing, as Mr. Webster put it, the impression made upon him only by the intensity with which he smoked. Mr. Webster could get no more at the first interview than the promise not to say No before he saw him again. At a second interview, with the aid of his own reflections and the urgency of leading members of the Bar and his own appeal, Mr. Webster got a reluctant assent. Mr. Webster used to add that, however the balance might be as to his public services, he was sure the Commonwealth owed him a great debt for that labor of love; that his efforts (so he thought) had secured for the State, for ~~twenty~~ years, so able, upright, and excellent a Chief Justice. It is not difficult to believe that the earnest counsel and pressure of Mr. Webster, fresh from the field of the great debate, — in which he had shown himself the first of living orators, and for which the heart of New England so clave to him, — should have had large, even decisive, influence upon the judgment and will of his friend. Be this as it may, it speaks none the less for the Chief Justice, that the greatest ot New England statesmen

should have felt it added to his laurels, and to his claims
upon the consideration of the people of Massachusetts,
that he had aided in obtaining for her the services of
such a magistrate.

We have stated these details of the life of the Chief
Justice before his appointment to the Bench, that we
might have some idea of his preparation for its duties.
In our view, his whole previous life was a preparation
and discipline and training for the work. The district schoolmaster, the usher of the Franklin School, the
writer for the Boston Gazette, the school committee-
man, the selectman, the representative in the General
Court, the editor of the Statutes, the framer of the City
Charter, as well as the advocate and counsellor of twenty-
six years, all went to make up the Chief Justice.

Chief Justice Shaw retired from the Bench in the summer of 1860, and died in the spring of 1861.

It remains for us to give some estimate of his judicial
life and labors. In this estimate we cannot omit the
element of time. He went upon the Bench in his fiftieth
year, and then worked, through the lifetime of a generation, with strength and vigor to the last. Some of his
later judgments are his best; are, indeed, remarkable for
their freshness, for the sagacity and grasp with which he
apprehended the new exigencies of society and business,
and applied and adapted old rules of law to them. A
striking and beautiful illustration may be found in the
case of the Commonwealth *vs.* Temple, 14 Gray, 69. This
opinion contains a thorough consideration of the rights
of travellers to the use of the highways, as affected and
modified by the introduction and use of street railways.
It was written when the Chief Justice was in the eightieth
year of his age. Old men travel well in beaten paths;
but this opinion strikes out new paths, and has the freshness, vigor, and constructive power of early manhood.
We never read it without admiration of the good sense,

tact, and grace even, with which the principles of the common law are moulded to new conditions, and the old fitted to the new, without seam. Lawyers in distant cities of the country, where street railroads were introduced, felt it to be fortunate that it should have fallen to the lot of Chief Justice Shaw to lay open this new path.

We have to consider, also, how broad and varied was the field of his labor; that the work which, in Westminster Hall, would be apportioned among at least a half-dozen different courts, is here united in one. Saving the jurisdiction in admiralty, his domain was the whole field of jurisprudence. To-day he would be sitting in a court of equity, to-morrow in a court of errors; the next day trying a capital indictment, the next the probate of a will; then a question of marriage or divorce, then an appeal in bankruptcy, — for the insolvent law of Massachusetts was in substance and effect a bankrupt law. Add to these the new domain of constitutional law, growing out of our written constitutions, State and national, and the limitations which they impose upon legislative, judicial, and executive authority, in the State or nation, the supervision of all courts of inferior jurisdiction, as well as for many purposes of municipal corporations, and you get some idea of the extent and variety of the labors of the court over which he presided. When we think of these, we marvel not that mistakes are sometimes made, but that they are not more frequently made; and that the decisions of a court having so boundless a field to cultivate and reap, should, for more than sixty years, compare well with those of any court whose jurisdiction and labors are limited to a single province of jurisprudence. The breadth and comprehensiveness of the field give breadth and comprehensiveness to the laborers; and cases are argued and settled less upon mere precedent and more upon principle, than in courts of more limited jurisdiction. If there is less accuracy of learning, there is less sticking in the bark, — more room for expansion and growth.

We may not omit to consider, in any estimate of the labors and services of the Chief Justice for thirty years, what vast changes have taken place in the methods and instrumentalities of commerce and business, and what new applications and modifications of the principles of the common law became necessary to meet the new exigencies.

It is a mistaken notion that, while everything moves forward, the law can remain stationary, or lag far behind. In no department of science, art, or business, have the changes been more marked, for the last thirty years, than in our jurisprudence. In the nature of things this could not be otherwise. Whenever a new invention or discovery is made, a new application of science to the arts and business of life, the law must follow close by in its footsteps, to secure its results, or to secure society against them. The first puff of the engine on the iron road announced a revolution in the law of bailments and of common carriers. The use of the railroad for the carriage of passengers and freight, has created a new branch of law, made up to some extent of statute provisions, but to a far greater extent by the application and adaptation of the rules of the common law to the new condition of things. The railroad began to be used as Judge Shaw came upon the Bench. How much his wisdom, foresight, and that clear comprehension of the principles of the common law, which enabled him to separate the rule from its old embodiments, and to mould it to new, contributed to build up this law, to give it system and harmony, and a substratum of solid sense, is well known to the profession. We refer to a single case, that of the Norway Plains Co. *vs.* Boston and Maine Railroad, 1 Gray, 263, as an illustration and confirmation of our position.

In the thirty years which Mr. Shaw presided in the Supreme Court, great changes were made in the jurisprudence of the State and the methods of administration; and he was constantly called upon to adapt himself to these changes, to reconcile the old with the new, and to assist in bringing them into order and harmony. As in the changes wrought in the law by new applications of science to intercommunication, he showed here also the strength and fertility of his resources, wherever principles and their application were involved.

We can but glance at the changes in the law and its administration.

In the methods of administration, the most important change is the extension of the equity jurisdiction and powers of the Supreme Court. When the Chief Justice came upon the Bench, the equity powers of the court were limited to a few clearly defined subjects-matter, and the equity business and practice were small. Before he left the Bench, its jurisdiction covered the whole domain of equity, and was fast acquiring the qualities of Aaron's rod.

In the common-law courts, a new system of pleading, except as to real actions, has been introduced, — as compared with the system of special pleading, illogical and slipshod, without form or comeliness; but, after all, answering the ends of substantial justice better than the often over-nice and subtle logic of the old system. With all the imperfections of the new practice, the merits of the cause sooner or later struggle into light.

There have been, also, most radical changes in the law of evidence. The objections to the competency of witnesses, with the discussions of which the reports were crowded thirty years ago, — as parties to the record, for interest direct or contingent in the suit, from want of religious belief, by reason of conviction for crime, even from the relation of husband and wife, — have been swept away, and, going only to the weight of the testimony, are transferred from the Bench to the jury-box.

Another material change is the abolition of imprisonment for debt, and of what was justly called the old grab-law, under which the maxim, " Vigilantibus non dormientibus subveniunt leges," was translated " The devil take the hindmost;" and the substitution for them of one of the best systems of insolvency and bankruptcy known to jurisprudence.

Most material also have been the changes in the law of the domestic relations, and especially that of husband and wife; by the most important of which the wife owns and controls the property coming to her by gift, descent, or as the fruit of her own labor, — a gift of power likely to lead to more radical results. Add to these, changes in the law of divorce, by which new causes for the dissolution of the marriage bond have been allowed, and the facility of separation greatly increased.

Nor would we omit, in any sketch of our legal progress, the changes in the modes of trying causes at *nisi prius* and in the arguments of questions of law *in banc;* that the manners of counsel have much less of asperity, that there is much less of personal controversy and identification of counsel with the passions and prejudices of their clients, than prevailed thirty years ago.

The rules requiring written or printed briefs and limiting the time for the argument of questions of law, and the limitation of the time for addressing the jury, have compelled counsel to greater directness and condensation of argument. This last change may have been wrought somewhat at the expense of the eloquence of the Bar. But this is not matter of serious regret. The court room is a place for serious business, and not for rhetoric; and any eloquence that does not arise from a direct, logical, earnest, condensed presentation of the cause, may well be left for the platform and the stump.

We have alluded to these changes in the law of Massachusetts and its practice, not to discuss them (we are indeed of opinion, that they have been wise and salutary), but for the purpose of indicating what constant vigilance, activity, and fresh power were necessary to the discharge of the duties of the Chief Justiceship for the period Mr. Shaw held the office. No following of the old ruts would answer. New paths had to be opened and fitted for travel, new hills of difficulty had to be cut through, new chasms bridged, new causeways over bog and morass constructed. In the comprehension of principles, new or old, and their adjustment and reconciliation, he was wise and strong. We do not think he took so kindly and readily to new forms of procedure; that he ever, for example, felt himself at home under the new Practice Act.

We must try to give a somewhat nearer view of the Chief Justice on the Bench. He was a good *nisi prius* judge. His perceptions were not remarkably rapid. He was not anxious to anticipate counsel, and see how summarily he could twist the neck of a cause. He was careful, thorough, systematic. He had a patient ear, — not merely the passive consent to listen, but the desire to be instructed in the facts and law of the case, no matter how inconsiderable the amount involved, or however humble the parties or their counsel. He was no respecter of persons; and a good point, well put by the youngest member of the Bar, told with the same effect as if by the leader. His rulings upon interlocutory questions and the admission of evidence were well considered and carefully noted. His charges to the jury were simple and clear; in difficult and complicated questions of law and fact, remarkably lucid, comprehensive, and forcible in matter and impressive in manner. He had a remarkable power of stating and illustrating the principles of law applicable to the cause so as to reach the minds of the jury. He was, in the best sense, impartial, and weighed with an even scale the merits of the cause. But he did not understand, that, to be impartial, he must have equal respect for truth and falsehood, or for a sound proposition and a fallacious one, or that the important points must not be stated with sufficient distinctness and force to be fully understood.

It was a pleasure to try causes before him, if it ever is a pleasure to try causes; for your repose in his integrity, fairness, and sense of justice was never ruffled. He held the reins in his own hands, quietly, firmly, with no twitching or jerking; but so that the strongest men at the Bar perfectly understood who presided.

The Chief Justice brought to the hearing *in banc* the same patience, the same desire to be instructed. There never was a judge who more thoroughly understood and appreciated the importance of an able, upright, and learned Bar in the administration of justice. He was very unwilling to decide any difficult cause that had not been thoroughly argued. He seemed to feel himself unqualified to decide it. He was reluctant even to depend upon briefs or written arguments. He liked far better the thorough oral discussion by counsel, with an occasional probing and feeling, on his own part, for the roots of the matters in controversy.

In his anxiety to do right, and his desire for the most thorough investigation and consideration of causes, the decision was sometimes deferred, after all the questions had been thoroughly and exhaustively discussed and considered, and when further delay might work injustice. Delay in judicial proceedings is not an unmixed evil. Some delay between the inception of a cause and the trial is good for the parties and the public. Many a bitter controversy has been spared, and the peace of many a family and neighborhood saved, by giving time for the passions of parties to cool and to pass in review before the judgment. And, when a cause has been tried, there is nothing that is so soothing to the failing party as the conviction, that he has been patiently heard, and his cause patiently and thoroughly considered. It is difficult to find the golden mean; but the delays of the Chief Justice, to those who did not understand the motive, looked like procrastination. If it was a failing, it leaned to virtue's side.

Chief Justice Shaw had the highest sense of natural justice and equity. But he had also the profoundest sense of the necessity of uniform and stable laws. He saw in the law the rule of conduct for the judge as well as the parties; and that it was the province of the good judge, as Lord Bacon says, *jus dicere*, not *jus dare*. He did not believe that it was any part of his duty to bend a positive rule of law to any fancied or even real equity of the case. He appreciated the wisdom and safety of positive rules and restrictions, like those of the Statute of Frauds and the Statute of Limitations; knowing they must sometimes work injustice, but were necessary safeguards against far greater wrongs, and, in the long run, wholesome and salutary. The subtleties and sentimentalities by which Chancellors have frittered away the Statute of Frauds — or, as Mr. Justice Story would say, rescued cases from its grasp — did not commend themselves to his judgment. He thought it better to say, This is the rule the lawmaker has prescribed.

He was a man of great firmness. It was not obstinacy, dogged conceit, unwillingness to confess error. He was singularly free from these. We never knew so great a man who had so little pride of opinion. His firmness was sense of duty; nothing could shake or disturb that. Such was the veneration for him, that no man would have ventured to suggest to him a consideration or motive outside of the line of duty. Though this firmness brought him into conflict with a strong and sensitive popular opinion on several occasions, we think it never impaired the public esteem and confidence. Men who knew Chief Justice Shaw found it impossible not to respect him.

It was the habit, while Chief Justice Shaw was on the Bench, for the court, on the last day of the law term or in long terms on Monday mornings, to deliver oral judgments in the cases already decided. Sometimes the reports of the opinions orally given sufficed. More frequently they were subsequently written out for the reporter. These were field days for the Chief Justice. He was never so great, and never felt to be so great, as in some of these oral judgments. His mind always seemed to be a little cramped by the pen. His oral style was not only more free ; it was, to our apprehension, more finished and perfect than his written. He had less to do with cases. Having made himself master of the facts and the precise points in contest, he applied to their solution the law, with such ease and clearness, that his law did not seem to you a thing acquired, but part of the mind itself.

Upon reading the judgments afterwards written out for the books, you felt a disappointment: a certain glow and finish were wanting. You could not help regretting that the oral judgment could not have been preserved fresh and warm as it fell from his lips.

The judicial opinion for which he was most bitterly and severely reproached was that in the Sims Case, 7 Cush. 285. There were portions of that opinion which did not command our assent. But it is not difficult to understand or to respect the position of the Chief Justice on the subject. In conviction and feeling he was firmly opposed to slavery, and to its extension. His article to the North American of 1820, shows the strength of these convictions. His opinions in Commonwealth vs. Ares, 18 Pick. 193, Commonwealth vs. Taylor, 3 Met. 72, Commonwealth vs. Fitzgerald, 7 Law Reporter, show clearly that, for the cause of natural right, he was ready to go up to the extremest line of positive law. The slave brought here by his master was free. The slave brought here by an officer of the navy, whose landing on our coast was involuntary, was free. He would not permit the voluntary return of a minor slave. He felt that in the Sims Case the line of positive law was reached; that it was defined by authority he was bound to respect. His own conviction, the result of maturest consideration, was, that the law was authorized by the Constitution of the United States; and that Constitution he had solemnly sworn to support. On its face was written, "This Constitution, and the laws of the United States made in pursuance thereof, . . . shall be the supreme law of the land, and the judges in every State shall be bound thereby; anything in the constitution and laws of any State to the contrary notwithstanding." The Chief Justice was so simple, honest, upright, and straightforward, it never occurred to him there was any way around, over, under, or through the barriers of the Constitution, — that is the only apology that can be made for him. When the passions of the hour have subsided, when the clouds of prejudice have been lifted, and reason re-ascends the steps of her throne, it will be sufficient.

But after all, the reputation of the Chief Justice as a jurist must rest upon his reported judicial opinions. These, beginning with the latter part of the ninth volume of Pickering, extend to, and will include, the sixteenth volume of Gray. They make, perhaps, a third part of the matter in these fifty-seven volumes. Through these reports he is known to the profession in this country and in Westminster Hall: but only to the profession. Few men read the reports but lawyers. The Bar constitutes the public of the Bench. The Bar only can fully appreciate the merits, or detect the shortcomings, of the judge. There is no escape from its judgment; and nothing but real merit secures its approbation. Pride of place, the air of gravity, parade of learning, solemn rhetoric, " wise saws and modern instances," avail nothing with good lawyers. They see at once whether the judge has got the matter in him, — such thorough comprehension of the principles of law, that they have ceased to be mere learning, and have become part of the mind's texture, — the analytic power which separates from the mass of immaterial matter the precise point at issue, and the trained judgment which applies to it the precise legal rule.

The judge is yet more severely tried in the reports. There is time for more careful analysis and thorough weighing of every position taken ; and when an opinion blocks the way of strong counsel, the dissection is merciless. The Chief Justice stood every test at the Bar. No lawyer practising before him doubted whether there was a strong man on the Bench. He will stand equally well in the reports. Take him for all in all, his is the first name in the judicial annals of Massachusetts. He had not, perhaps, the legal genius of Parsons or Jackson, but, it seems to the writer, larger grasp and wider scope.

His judicial opinions are thorough and exhaustive. They seldom rest on mere authority, but strike down to the hard-pan, — to the principle on which the cases rest. Considered as judgments merely, the range of discussion is sometimes too broad. The reader has to be cautious and careful to discern between what is necessarily involved in the decision, and what comes from his overflowing mind in the way of illustration and argument.

There was another quality of the mind of the Chief Justice, which always impressed us, — its forecast, a sort of prophetic forecast. It never said to itself, Settle this point, and "Sufficient unto the day is the evil thereof." His was " the wise discourse, which looks *before* and after." His mind was constantly reaching and feeling its way forward. His opinions show this habit of thought, and frequently contain intimations and suggestions which you find in subsequent cases have ripened into rules. A mind like this, it is obvious, would not be content simply to find a point upon which a case could be decided or turned off. It insisted upon grasping the principles involved, and wheeling the case into line.

We venture to affirm, that there are, in the reports of this country or of Westminster Hall, no more instructive and suggestive judicial opinions and arguments than those of Judge Shaw. When, in the course of professional investigation, we strike one of his leading opinions, there is a feeling of comfort, an assurance that, if we do not find our point decided, we shall at least be refreshed and strengthened and directed for our farther journey. We know of no more valuable contributions to the illustration of the principles of the common law.

While the style of the Chief Justice is vigorous, forcible, and copious in illustration, terseness and precision are sometimes wanting. Chief Justice Shaw could not have written Vice-Chancellor Wigram's Treatise on the Use of Extrinsic Evidence in the Interpretation of Wills, or the opinion of his own court in the case of Brattle Square Church vs. Grant; in both of which the law assumes the beauty and precision of the exact sciences. , But though there is here and there a little diffuseness, and sometimes repetition, the points are clearly and thoroughly put, and vigorously enforced. He did not wind his way through the entanglement of glade and forest. He cut through a broad path, and let in the air and sunlight. It took time ; but the way afterward was open and clear, and its direction not to be mistaken.

It is, of course, impracticable to examine, within any reasonable limits, even the leading opinions of the Chief Justice. To be fairly judged, they must be carefully analyzed and studied. Examine almost any volume, and we may get some idea of the extent of the field in which he had to labor, of the thoroughness of his work, and of the largeness of his powers. We have before us the seventh volume of Cushing (1853). The volume contains at least three leading and most important causes, in which the opinion of the Court was given by the Chief Justice, — Commonwealth vs. Alger, May vs. Breed and the Sims Case. We shall but refer to them.

Commonwealth *vs.* Alger was an indictment for constructing and maintaining a wharf extending beyond the lines fixed by the statutes of the Commonwealth for Boston Harbor. The defendant (Alger) was, under the colony ordinance, the owner of the fee in the flats on which the wharf was built.

The Acts of the Legislature fixing the lines of the harbor, and restraining the owners of the flats from building beyond those lines, had made no provision for compensation to the owners, on account of such restriction. The case was argued for the defendant with great ability and force, upon the ground that the act in question was an exercise of the right of eminent domain and taking of private property for public use; and that, no compensation having been provided, the act, as against the defendant, was invalid, as contravening the Bill of Rights of Massachusetts, Art. 10, and the provision of the Constitution of the United States, forbidding a State to pass a law impairing the obligation of contracts.

The case opened two important questions, — the rights of owners of land bounding on the sea to the flats over which the tide ebbs and flows; and, secondly, the power of the Legislature to regulate the use and enjoyment of these rights. If the reading of this opinion should leave any doubt as to the profound learning of the Chief Justice, his grasp of principles, or his great power of illustrating and applying them, no argument of ours would remove it.

In May *vs.* Breed, the Chief Justice discusses the question whether a discharge, under the English bankrupt law, of a debt due to a citizen of Massachusetts, but contracted in England and payable there, is a bar to an action on the debt in that State; and holding that the law of the place where the contract is made and to be performed gives it its character, measures its obligations, and settles when and how it shall be terminated and discharged, pronounces the judgment of the Court for the defendant.

Sims' Case, as before observed, is an elaborate discussion of the constitutionality of the Fugitive Slave Law of 1850.

Though the Chief Justice presided over a local tribunal, these cases indicate how comprehensive was its jurisdiction, and that no court where the common law is administered could be called upon to discuss and settle questiohs of greater magnitude and difficulty. Is it too much to ask, Is there any court upon which the opinions in Commonwealth *vs.* Alger and May *vs.* Breed would not have reflected new lustre and honor?

The manners of the Chief Justice upon the Bench were quiet, simple, dignified. There was, however, an occasional austerity and roughness, which, to those who did not know him, looked like acerbity of temper. It was not so. The Chief Justice had a kind heart which would not willingly give pain. We think the remarks of his distinguished successor give us the true explanation of this occasional roughness of manner: —

"It is a great mistake to suppose," says Mr. Chief Justice Bigelow, " that it had its origin in any unkindness of feeling or acerbity of temper. It arose rather from the pre-occupation of his mind with the weight of thought, care, and responsibility with which it was burdened, and which made him, at times, insensible to his manner of speech. The best evidence of this is, that he seemed to be unconscious that his mode of address ever gave cause of offence, or inflicted an injury upon the feelings " (1 Allen 605–6).

But it was a fault. The practice of law has trials and vexations enough, without adding any that are unnecessary. The utmost courtesy and respect are required from the Bar to the Bench; and courtesy is a reciprocal virtue. The example, too, of so great a judge is dangerous, and may tempt others to the fault, without the great qualities that redeem it.

If we might, for a moment and for a closing word,
forget the critic and speak as the friend, it would be to
say that, great as was the judge, the man was greater
than the magistrate, — Lemuel Shaw than the venerable
Chief Justice. A truer man, indeed, did not grace his
generation. With that little roughness of exterior, he
was like the nuggets of California, — through and through
solid gold.

But the man bowed to the magistrate. With the largest sense of equity, he was the servant of the law he was
set to administer, and obeyed its mandate. With the
most generous love of freedom and hatred of oppression,
he stood unflinchingly by the Constitution he had sworn
to support. With the soundest judgment, with masterly
powers of reasoning, and, in discussion, with a subtlety of
logic seldom equalled, he had literally no pride of opinion,
but retained to the last the docility of childhood, — the
ever open and receptive and waiting spirit, into which
wisdom loves to come and take up its abode. With a
stern sense of justice, he had the tenderness of a woman;
and while the magistrate pronounced the dread sentence of the law, the man was convulsed with grief and
sympathy.

With a firm trust in God, with a constant sense of his
presence, looking to him for guidance and support, nothing could move him from the path of duty. He stood in
his place, and the billows broke at his feet.

As man and as judge, he stood the severest test, the
closest scrutiny. The nearer you got to him, the more
thoroughly you knew him, — the greater, wiser, better
man and magistrate he appeared to you. Great on the
Bench and in the books, it was in the consultation room
that you first understood and felt the variety and afflu-
ence and extent of his resources.

CPSIA information can be obtained
at www.ICGtesting.com
Printed in the USA
BVHW040907281118
534010BV00038B/489/P

9 780483 557062